Playing Scared

Playing Scared

My Journey Through Stage Fright

Sara Solovitch

BLOOMSBURY

LONDON · OXFORD · NEW YORK · NEW DELHI · SYDNEY

Bloomsbury Publishing
An imprint of Bloomsbury Publishing Plc

50 Bedford Square   1385 Broadway
London   New York
WC1B 3DP   NY 10018
UK   USA

www.bloomsbury.com

BLOOMSBURY and the Diana logo are trademarks of Bloomsbury Publishing Plc

First published in Great Britain 2015

British Library Cataloguing-in-Publication Data
A catalogue record for this book is available from the British Library.

ISBN: HB: 978-1-4088-5455-6
       ePub: 978-1-4088-5456-3

2 4 6 8 10 9 7 5 3 1

Typeset by RefineCatch Ltd, Bungay, Suffolk
Printed and bound in Great Britain by CPI Group (UK) Ltd, Croydon CR0 4YY

For Rich

CONTENTS

INTRODUCTION

For most of my adult life, virtually no one—not even my closest friends—knew I played the piano. And that was how I wanted it. Playing the piano had once defined me, but so, too, had my stage fright. I was the kind of pianist who played well when there was nothing at stake: in my parents' house, at my lesson, behind closed doors. But put me in front of an audience and my hands would ice over while some invisible spigot let loose a burst of sweat that soaked my palms and fingers. When I quit at nineteen, my parents protested that I was giving up the best part of myself. You'll go back to it one day, they predicted. When I finally did, more than thirty years had passed. Word got around; my husband bragged about it at the office, and one winter evening in 2011, I found myself at a cheery holiday party, being exhorted to play something, anything, on the host's baby grand. I demurred. The host jovially insisted. I declined. The other guests cajoled. I said no. After opening the piano bench, the host pulled out a book of Bach inventions. How about this, he said. Yes, yes, play that, the others chanted. Jump! Jump! was what I heard.

In that moment, I realized nothing had changed. I was fifty-six years old and my stage fright was as fearsome and powerful as when I was fourteen—maybe more so. If I had just sat down and played, it would have been a forgettable moment. Nobody would have cared if I had made a mistake. Instead, their pleas and my refusals lasted longer than a two-page invention.

Stage fright, or performance anxiety, is both utterly mysterious, an act of mutiny by the mind against the body, and ludicrously commonplace, as ordinary as the common cold. It is the kind of condition for which people inevitably trot out the names of famous sufferers, the way they do for Asperger syndrome or bipolar disorder. As if to say . . . what, exactly? That a diagnosis is not the end of the world? That you or your loved one is in good company? A *Who's Who of Stage Fright* makes for an imposing roster, one that includes Hugh Grant (who's considered quitting acting), Paul McCartney (who once said he "nearly gave up the Beatles" because of it), and Adele (who has projectile vomited onstage). The guitarist Andrés Segovia confessed that his very bones shook before a concert. He told himself that stage fright was a sign of talent and quoted no less an authority than Sarah Bernhardt. The world's most acclaimed actress was a self-described *traqueuse*—someone prone to attacks of *le trac*, or stage fright. So too was the pianist Vladimir Horowitz, who once took a twelve-year break from concertizing. To tame his stage fright, he maintained a rigid regimen on perform-ance days, always eating the same meal of Dover sole and asparagus, which often had to be specially flown in. By one account, three burly men were required to drag him from his dressing room as he fought, begged, and screamed, before literally tossing him onto the stage. Horowitz reportedly gave some of his finest performances under such circumstances.[1]

The list goes on: Barbra Streisand, Laurence Olivier, Bette Midler, Maria Callas, Stephen Fry, Ella Fitzgerald, Jesse Eisenberg, Enrico Caruso, Rod Stewart, Mel Gibson, Luciano Pavarotti, Brian Wilson, Carol Burnett.[2]

Mention stage fright and chances are good that someone will cite a 1973 survey, first reported in the London *Sunday Times*, that identified public speaking as the most common fear in America.[3] Respondents said they would rather be plagued by insects and suffer financial ruin than stand before an audience, open their mouths, and talk. The survey became a source for late-night comedy routines and took on a life of its own. When Jerry Seinfeld joked that more people at a funeral would rather be in the coffin than give the eulogy, that's what people remembered. It lodged itself in the collective unconscious, where it's remained ever since, to be summoned up and quoted as if it were a fact of life.

Stage fright is the great leveler, cutting down prophets, presidents, musicians, actors, dancers, lawyers, athletes, preachers, rabbis, teachers, CEOs, salesmen, advertising reps—anyone who has ever had to stand up in front of a group and *do* something.

It demanded some kind of reckoning, I found myself thinking as I picked my way through a Bach prelude one evening in May 2012. If I could give myself a year to research the science and psychology of stage fright, try out various therapies, and persuade performance coaches and sport psychologists to work with me, maybe I could beat this thing. I would find a teacher who would not only train me as a pianist, but also help me as a performer. I would practice hours every day, quash my fears, and at the end of the year play a recital for an audience of fifty or more people. The idea emerged full-blown, like Athena from Zeus's head. It terrified me, but I couldn't turn away from it.

Sara at twenty-one months old (Author's family photo)

This book chronicles my quest to understand and overcome a lifetime of stage fright. I have practiced meditation (fitfully) and yoga (faithfully). I have explored a variety of therapies: exposure therapy, cognitive behavior therapy, biofeedback, EMDR (Eye Movement Desensitization and Reprocessing), breathing coordination, hypnosis, and (that mainstay of musicians) the Alexander technique. I've read what Sigmund Freud, Carl Jung, Alfred Adler, and Joseph Weiss had to say about performance anxiety and tried to glean a few of the rewards. I've interviewed neuroscientists about their research into fear and the brain—specifically, how the brain can be retrained to excise fear, that most primal of emotions. Scientists today understand the workings of fear better than any other emotion. They know where it is sparked in the brain and how to elicit it in athletes, students, test takers, and anyone willing to enter the lab and receive an unpleasant but harmless electric shock. Yet it's the simple beta-blocker, first marketed in 1962 for the treatment of angina and heart disease, that remains the standby for so many of us with performance anxiety. When I asked my doctor for a prescription, her response was one of immediate recognition: "Oh, the public-speaking pill!" Turned out she used it herself.

Along the way, I met other performance-haunted people who steadied me, cautioned me, inspired me, and shared their tales: the major league second baseman who couldn't find first base; the Baptist preacher for whom every week was a countdown to Sunday; the lawyer who feared she was getting lockjaw whenever she stood to give a speech; the onetime child star from the New York stage who moved to Los Angeles for a role in a 1970s TV sitcom, then froze on camera, unable to remember his character's name. Anyone whose hands have turned wet with sweat or whose voice has cracked and faltered when standing before an audience can relate.

Chapter 1

THE AGONY OF MY ECSTASY

A T THE ANNUAL MUSIC festival in Port Colborne, the small Ontario town where I grew up, my fellow competitors knew me as the one who could be counted on to crash and burn. My piano teacher, Mrs. Wolfenden, was convinced otherwise. Each spring, starting when I was ten, she plotted which Bach invention or Mozart sonata I should perform, promising that I was sure to get over my nerves now that I was a whole year older. My mother, for her part, didn't need any convincing. According to her, all I needed to do was practice more.

It never occurred to me that I could refuse, even when I was fourteen and Mrs. Wolfenden declared that I was ready for a more serious competition, requiring a forty-minute drive to the neighboring city of St. Catharines. This time, I told myself, it was going to be different. My fingers knew the music so cold, it wouldn't matter what I thought about or if I thought at all. Waiting my turn in the front row—that no-man's-land between performer and audience—I affected interest in the pianist onstage, closed my eyes, and tapped out the opening bars of the Mozart Sonata no. 8 in A Minor. But as the simple triad shifted to a four-note chord, I grew aware that the bottoms of my thighs had gone clammy and my palms were already getting wet. I rubbed them into my jumper, but—just my luck—I was wearing wool, a natural water repellent. Now the audience was clapping and, looking up, I saw the girl taking her bow, moving confidently toward the stairs. I knew her, or, more accurately, I knew her piano playing. Her name was Nancy, and she never missed a note. But she played woodenly—like a cold brick, my mother said, though I suspected she admired the girl's cool demeanor. I glanced behind me, trying to search out my mother in the crowd. There was a blur of faces, all aimed in my direction.

Pushing myself out of my chair, I felt my thighs cling to the wood. I brushed past Nancy on the stairs and tried to smile, but my mouth was dry. And now, I realized, my hands were sopping wet. When I sat on the piano bench, I became aware that my knees were knocking and my feet were shaking.

I waited for the shaking to die, and when it didn't, I closed my eyes and tried to conjure up what my piano teacher once suggested: an image of myself playing for a barnyard full of animals. The room had grown silent. I looked down at my hands, which, for a fourteen-year-old, were unusually muscular, the result of years of practicing scales, Hanon and Czerny exercises, and Bach inventions. But the hands were small, too small for many of the larger chords in the music I was starting to play, and sometimes I hated them the way other girls my age hated their small breasts. They were peasant hands, short-fingered, like those of my father and everyone on his side of the family. It didn't help that I regularly bit my fingernails down to the quick. I also gnawed at my cuticles and chewed on the ends of pencils, a habit that earned me the school-yard epithet Eager Beaver. Lately, I had been picking away at the skin around the fourth finger of my left hand. It had gotten infected and a throbbing abscess developed, so that every time I touched a key the pain sounded an alarm, warning me to stay away. Just a few days earlier, my mother had sent me to our family doctor, who lanced the boil, releasing a spray of mustard-yellow pus.

My last thought, as I lifted my hands, was that the finger had almost fully healed. And then I leaned in and, with a grace note slur from D sharp to E, jumped into what I liked to think of as a horse race. Some music waits to unfold and lets you slowly wrap your mind around it, but not this piece. As my left hand played the triad like a steady canter, I let myself hum along to the melody—a low drone just loud enough to quell the shaking. My brain was jumping as fast as my fingers and my hands knew the rules and miraculously obeyed. It sounded good, I realized, maybe better than good. If I could keep playing at this speed, the air might even dry my hands.

But as I came to the end of the first theme—a series of fast octave jumps, Cs to Gs to Cs—my wet fingers went sliding. I stopped for an instant, but a discernible instant. I was never one of those pianists who could glide past mistakes and make them invisible to all but the most knowledgeable listeners. I halted, then resumed, and for a while I was once again able to forget everything but the music, my fingers plunging into the densest passages of the piece. This was the part I loved, and for a few moments I was able to enter Mozart's world. Sometimes I thought these passages were the only thing that could explain myself to me, but as I moved through the music, or the music moved through me, some almost imperceptible signal registered in my brain, and I remembered where I was, remembered the adjudicator who was sitting alone in a gray suit at a table in the aisle, scratching silently with his pencil. My mother was there, too, hidden somewhere in the audience. She was listening attentively, critically, while, just where I could see them from the corner of my eye, my competitors hovered expectantly in the front row like—and now it dawned on me exactly whom they reminded me of—Madame Defarge and her fellow *tricoteuses* from *A Tale of Two Cities*, sitting back with their needles and yarn, knitting and watching greedily as the guillotine did its job.

That image precipitated another slip, but now I was close to the end and I pushed on to the place where my fingers dashed through a long run of notes like a sparkler going off. The lanced finger was tolling its own internal alarm bell: *Boil, boil, toil and trouble.* The final chords were here now, demanding their due, and then the piece was over.

I gave a hurried bow and rushed off the stage, searching out my mother as I headed toward my seat. The audience rushed by like trees along the highway when my father drove fast, passing every car just for the hell of it and yelling at me to get my arm inside unless I wanted to lose it. I wondered if it was because I was walking so fast, or were there tears in my eyes? I groped for my seat, and though I knew it was childish, that she would hate it, I couldn't help myself: I turned back and sought out my mother's face. When at last I lit on it, she refused to look at me. She sat erect, her posture as always ramrod straight, staring ahead in the middle of a crowded row. I asked her with my eyes the only thing I cared about— *Are you mad at me?*—but she looked determinedly away, watching the boy who was next up onstage.

He was unknown to me, with a foreign-looking name, Kiran or something similar, and he was wonderful. Finally, here was someone who, even under pressure, played with the love I felt when I played by myself. I was so moved that, for once, I didn't feel envy. What I thought was that I would happily gain fifty pounds if I could just make the piano sing like that. At that moment, it was the most valuable thing I could imagine for trade. A few months earlier, I had entered puberty and blossomed from a gawky kid with braids into a pudgy teenager with breasts. These days, when I came down to breakfast in a flannel nightgown, my parents almost in one breath urged me to go upstairs and "cover up." The extra pounds clearly bothered my svelte mother, who referred to them as "big ones." As in, "It looks like you've gained a few big ones." The fantasy that I might trade fifty pounds to play like *that*—and without stage fright—seemed a good exchange.

Kiran was the last person to play, and for a long time after he finished, the adjudicator continued making notes. Now that the music was over, the scratch of his pencil filled the hall. At last, he approached and stood in front of us, a slight man who, with his thin hair and sharpened features, looked like Fred Astaire. He talked about the importance of performing and playing, but I knew it had nothing to do with me, and when he mentioned Kiran's name and everyone applauded, I clapped along. The adjudicator talked some more, and then I thought I heard my name. I couldn't be sure, though. I had had a similar experience many times in school, where I habitually sat with a book open on my lap, just under the desktop, so immersed in the story and the characters that the teacher would sometimes call my name two or three times before I responded, not looking up until the sound of laughter broke the spell. It was like being under water.

Now, looking up, I realized with surprise that I had been named second-place winner. Apparently, the audience also was surprised. A noise like a collective gasp moved through the room, and the adjudicator raised a hand as if to stem a political revolt. Yes, he said, his voice loud now, she made mistakes. That is why she didn't get first place. But she played the most musically of anyone here. It matters little if a musician plays perfectly but without feeling. And with that pronouncement, he beckoned me forward and presented me with a silver medal.

I was not nearly as gratified as my mother. She saw the prize—and more important, the adjudicator's remarks—as vindication of everything that she had long been claiming for me. Her delight knew no bounds after she discovered that the adjudicator, Harold Weiss, was a member of the faculty of Eastman School of Music in Rochester, where her older sister, Madeline—my aunty Maddy—had once trained as a concert pianist. He had declared that I was "really musical," and who recognized talent better than an Eastman professor? I was of course glad that I had made my mother so proud, but it didn't seem like such a big deal. I might even have forgotten the whole episode if it had ended there. But its real significance would become clear only in retrospect.

Mother, Sara, brother Joseph, and Aunty Maddy (Author's family photo)

Two years after the competition in St. Catharines, when I was sixteen, my family—me, my brother, sister, and mother—moved into my aunt's house in Hornell, a dreary town tucked in the Allegheny Mountains of western New York, about seventy-five miles from Rochester. Only my father stayed behind in Ontario, with the vague promise that he would follow as soon as he sold his furniture store. Though the town was bleak, the house was a country in and of itself, a mansion with a personality that seemed to shape our relationships. Stepping into its vestibule was, to us, who had never seen

Europe, as good as entering Versailles. We immediately removed our shoes because the floors of every room, except for the kitchen and bathrooms, were covered with beautiful Oriental rugs. The library was filled with leather-bound volumes of classic literature and out-of-date business tomes, and the top ledges of the bookshelves were lined with ivory busts of Greek gods and goddesses.

The parlor was so large that Aunty Maddy's Steinway grand took up what seemed like a mere nook, and there were clocks everywhere: a porcelain clock from eighteenth-century France, hand-painted with fleurs-de-lis, that kept silent time and an enormous grandfather clock that ticked loudly and boomed the quarter hour, following you up the heavy staircase, past the landing with its stained-glass windows of the rising sun and looming moon, into the Queen's Room, as we called it, where Aunty Maddy slept alone, ever since the death of Uncle Benny five years earlier, and the Princess Room, where my mother also now slept alone in a canopied bed.

When the sisters were together, everyone else was excluded. The two of them would disappear upstairs and sit on Maddy's bed, poring over her treasures of gold and diamonds that she kept locked away in a brown leather traveler's bag inside her closet. With the doors closed and the curtains drawn, the two sisters sealed off the world. They had grown up poor; their father had lost everything in the Depression, and my mother had combed the hills when she was a young girl, gathering dandelion greens for dinner. But Maddy, who was the oldest, had always had a penchant for making money. Whenever she babysat her little sister, she made a game of searching out pennies and nickels below the curbs and trapped beneath the street grates. Maddy had luck, and she was generous with it. My mother, Polly, revered her. Though the move to Hornell clearly fulfilled her deepest wish, to be with her sister, it also suited her musical ambitions for me. For Maddy announced that she intended to send me to Eastman's preparatory department. I was to be given opportunities I would never have had if we stayed in Port Colborne.

Before the beginning of the school year, my mother called Eastman and asked to speak to Mr. Weiss, reminding him of my performance a couple of years earlier in St. Catharines. Yes, he said, he did in fact remember it. He remembered me. And he agreed to take me on as a student. Which meant that every Saturday morning, I would leave Aunty Maddy's house at seven o'clock, catch the bus in front of the little Greyhound storefront a block away, change buses in Dansville twenty miles away, and arrive in Rochester by ten. My lesson began at eleven, and when I knocked on Mr. Weiss's studio door, he greeted me in his neat gray suit with a polite wave of the hand.

One of the first things he said when I walked into his studio, swinging the stiff calfskin "music case" that my aunt had bought me, was that my days of competition were over. For the next two years, until I turned eighteen and went off to college, I would spend Saturdays taking lessons, studying music history, theory, counterpoint, and harmony, participating in school recitals, playing in Eastman's grand concert hall, and giving the occasional demonstration to visiting piano teachers in his studio.

Mr. Weiss emphasized technique. He could easily devote half the lesson to drilling me on scales, arpeggios, and diminished sevenths, and I practiced them at home at least an hour every day. My fingers flew. His ban on competition had eased some of my anxiety. There were annual evaluations before the head of the preparatory department and recitals in the grand concert hall, but these were low-key affairs compared with the frenzied competitions of my childhood. I liked to wander through the conservatory's basement, listening to the din of scales, fugues, sonatas, and études that filtered out of the practice rooms and into the hallway. I could usually find an empty room where I, too, could practice or, more likely, crack open *Dombey and Son* or whatever Dickens novel I was reading at the time.

The last performance I ever gave was at my graduation recital in May 1971. It was a program of all the preparatory students, each of us required to play just one piece. Mine was Brahms's Intermezzo in A Major, a dark and introspective work. From Brahms to Dickens, I loved everything to do with the nineteenth century, and I played well. When it was over, I relaxed in my seat. A violinist was now onstage, someone I recognized from my music appreciation class. She was playing a Mozart violin sonata, and I knew at once that her playing—her tone, her phrasing, her passion—was on a different order of magnitude from mine. I was reminded of Kiran, the pianist who had made such an enormous impression four years earlier. I knew in an instant that I could never play like this girl, no matter how much I practiced or how flawlessly I executed. That instant of comprehension was both transformative and distressing.

Father, Mother, and Aunty Maddy (Author's family photo)

I had played well enough to reignite the two sisters' ambitions, however. For as soon as I left the recital hall, I saw them in a huddle with Mr. Weiss in the middle of the lobby. My mother motioned me over. "Would you like to go to Eastman's instead of university?" she asked. "Mr. Weiss thinks—"

I didn't wait to hear the rest. "Absolutely not," I said. I had my own plans. I was going to become a writer. At that moment, I didn't care if I ever played the piano again. It felt final—like leaving the church, turning away from the faith, and becoming a lapsed Catholic or nonobservant Jew. It was years before I understood how deeply music had permeated my identity, years before I recognized that the word *practice* had a wider meaning than time spent at the piano. It was almost an epiphany when, as an adult, I realized that the word was commonly used in connection with religion. But now I was eighteen and could worship—or not—wherever and whatever I chose.

Chapter 2

BLINDED BY THE LIGHT:
A SHORT HISTORY

IN MY SENIOR YEAR of college, I lived across the hall
from a guy who wore desert boots and bright-colored
T-shirts under his denim button-downs. I could always tell
when he was around by the loud jazz that wafted out of
his room. When I finally got up my nerve to knock on his
door and ask about the record he was playing (Don Pullen's
Solo Piano Album), we became friends. I quickly learned that
he was a music obsessive who had gone to Columbia College
for one reason: to work at the university radio station,
WKCR-FM, the beacon of New York City's progressive jazz
scene. When we met, Rich was its president.

He and his compatriots at the station were like political
revolutionaries, except that their cause was jazz. They saw
themselves as deliverers of the truth, changing the world
through the music of underappreciated geniuses such as
Charles Mingus, Ornette Coleman, Sam Rivers, McCoy
Tyner, and scores of others. Rich spent his four years at college
hosting jazz shows, presenting live concerts, organizing on-air

festivals, and interviewing musicians. His classwork was secondary. After I began accompanying him to concerts, I was sometimes disquieted by the extent of his immersion. When the music began, he fell through a looking glass into another world. It seemed to leave him in a daze. He had an unerring ear; just one note of a recording and he instantly recognized the musician. I'd never known anybody who could do that. One day before the end of the final semester, he walked in on me as I was playing Debussy's *The Girl with the Flaxen Hair* in an empty room on campus. I, too, was totally immersed. That was the moment, he says, he knew I was the one.

When I graduated that spring, Aunty Maddy gave me a Baldwin upright. Over the years, I lugged it around from Brooklyn to Buffalo, Washington, and Philadelphia, before landing in Santa Cruz, California. The instrument was a part of my identity. I had stopped thinking of myself as any kind of pianist. I'd whited out that part of me; months and sometimes years went by when I hardly touched the keyboard. But though I had never considered becoming a professional musician—I wasn't good enough, I didn't want to work that hard—I took it as a given that the piano would remain a part of my life.

Music was a constant presence in our house. Rich—we married a few years after college—went on to become a newspaper music critic. All three of our sons were musically gifted, with perfect or relative pitch. Yet my own musical life ebbed away; I returned to the piano ever more infrequently, and usually only when my family cleared out and I had a few moments to myself. That's when I would try to find my way back to an old piece, like one of the Mozart sonatas I used to love. I was playing the A minor K. 310, one day when Rich and the kids burst in from some outing. Max, who was then about six, rushed to the piano and flung his arms around my waist, buried his head in my lap, and cried, "Oh, Mommy, that is so beautiful! Why don't you always play for us?"

Why indeed? Why was it so painful to play before a modest little audience—my family, say—when I could speak before large groups of people? Why did it feel as though my whole being were laid out on the piano's soundboard for everyone to pick at? What was really at stake here?

To my relief, none of my sons exhibited any fear onstage. Two of them would go on to become professional musicians— one a classical violinist, the other a jazz saxophonist. For years, I attended their recitals, at first anxious and then

Ben, Rich, Sara, Max, and Jesse (in front) (Author's family photo)

bemused, proud, and maybe a little envious of their natural stage presence. They seemed to come alive and play best while performing. When Max was seven years old and hardly more than a beginner on the violin, he played with such intensity at a student recital that two fathers sought him out afterward to thank him and share, almost shyly, that he had made them cry.

I used to get nervous just waiting for the boys to play in public, but after a while their aplomb lulled me into a state of confidence. Then, one day, I attended a recital of first-place winners for the local music teachers' association. Max was playing Fritz Kreisler's Praeludium and Allegro, but before he had his turn, a girl of twelve or thirteen went onstage to play a Bach prelude and fugue. From the moment she sat down at the keyboard, she began having serious memory lapses, staring blank-eyed into the piano's guts before resuming and failing again. All my old fears came flooding back. I grabbed the seat of my chair and clung tight, as if I were on a carnival ride. I didn't know where to put my eyes; I felt as though I had swallowed a chicken bone. I imagined, when I allowed myself to look, that she even resembled the adolescent me: braids, glasses, gawky. I didn't feel sorry for her; I wanted her to disappear. *Get her off the stage*, I wanted to scream at her parents. *How dare she do this?* When the recital ended and we were getting out of our seats, I debated whether I should go up to her and her family and say something, share my own history of terrible performances, and assure her that it wasn't the end of the world. There was a little group of well-wishers gathered around her, but I couldn't bring myself to join them. I didn't want to be within touching distance. Max had played with his usual insouciance, and I wanted to associate myself with him, to pretend that I couldn't imagine what it was like to be anything but confident in oneself.

But even that wasn't to last forever. When Max was almost through college, having majored in French and literature, he announced—late for a violinist—that he wanted to pursue a career in classical music. He graduated, moved back home, and resumed his studies with his beloved violin teacher, practicing six and seven hours a day in an effort to catch up with the conservatory students who had committed themselves to this path from a young age. He managed to get into a good conservatory—the Glenn Gould School in Toronto—but almost overnight his confidence disappeared, supplanted by a fear that overpowered him even at his weekly lessons. Now that he actually cared, that he had some skin in the game, he was no longer nonchalant. For the next two years, as I watched and listened to him agonize about this sudden new intimacy with stage fright, I felt as though I had passed on a bad gene.

The oldest account of stage fright on record has to be the story of Moses, who expressed understandable anxiety when asked by God to lead the Israelites out of Egypt. He wasn't the man for the job, he protested. Who would listen to him? He was a poor speaker. He stuttered. "Slow of speech and of a slow tongue," he described himself in that first conversation at the burning bush. God wasn't buying. "Who gave you a mouth to talk with," He pointedly asked, before relenting: "Isn't Aaron your brother? He's pretty good with words." Thus Aaron became the front man and Moses his ventriloquist.[1]

Several thousand years went by before the next reported case of stage fright. According to a story told by Carl Jung, it took place in ancient Athens, where Socrates was grooming his protégé Alcibiades to be the most celebrated orator and statesman of his time. As a young man, Alcibiades was incapacitated by a fear of public speaking. Socrates accompanied him on long walks through the streets of Athens, introducing him first to a blacksmith, then to a shoemaker, asking if he was afraid of the one and then the other. When Alcibiades answered no and then no again, Socrates demanded, "Then why should you be afraid of the people of Athens? They consist of those people, they are nothing but faces."[2]

It was Mark Twain who coined the term *stage fright*, and though he claimed to have experienced it only once, it must have been a memorable experience, given the devastating portrayal in *The Adventures of Tom Sawyer*. The scene takes place at the end of the school year, when Tom is required to deliver the "Give me liberty or give me death" speech before an audience of parents, teachers, and students. The cocky boy is quickly reduced to a puddle of jelly:

> A ghastly stage-fright seized him, his legs quaked under him and he was like to choke. True, he had the manifest sympathy of the house but he had the house's silence, too, which was even worse than its sympathy. The master frowned, and this completed the disaster. Tom struggled awhile and then retired, utterly defeated. There was a weak attempt at applause, but it died early.[3]

The term *stage fright* has come under occasional challenge, since fear of the *stage* isn't really the issue. A terror of performance can strike anywhere. But unlike other terms used to describe the condition—social phobia, cold feet, chicken heart, the jitters, glossophobia (fear of speaking in public), communication apprehension, paruresis (fear of urinating in the presence of others), the yips (in baseball, cricket, basketball, and tennis), dartitis (in darts), target panic (archery), the schneid (a losing streak in cards, sports, or dating), and the Thing, not to mention biting the apple and plain old performance anxiety—"stage fright" conveys that deer-in-the-headlights feeling that escorts people to the podium, the playing field, and the stage.

Standing in the spotlight, one struggles to counter the feeling of being exposed, of feeling naked and alone. Hip-hop musician Jay-Z got to the heart of it in a 2010 interview on NPR's *Fresh Air*, when host Terry Gross asked why rappers grab at their crotches. It was more than straight-out vulgarity, he responded. It was about young men onstage, often for the first time in their lives, looking out at an ocean of fans and feeling naked and scared to death. "So when you feel naked, what's the first thing you do?" he said. "You cover yourself."[4]

In the twenty-first century's age of anxiety, everything is performance: "Work, play, sex, and even [political] resistance—it's all performance to us," writes new media theorist Jon McKenzie in *Perform or Else*, a quasi-academic study that links artistic, organizational, and technological performances.[5] Performance, he observes, is the filter through which we consider every imaginable product: "high performance" cars, stereos, lawn mowers, toilet paper, and missile systems. The world has become a "test site" in "an age of global perform-ance," from art and spectacle to Wall Street warfare and air fresheners. Anthropologists have analyzed the rituals of indi-genous peoples as performance; sociologists have applied the word to describe everyday social interactions from the way one nods hello to a silent flirtation; cultural theorists have examined race, gender, and social politics in terms of performance.

Contemporary culture presupposes performance, a put-up-or-shut-up mind-set in which virtually every activity, from the banal to the most intimate, is photographed, documented, videotaped, and evaluated. The zeitgeist begins with birth, an experience now often celebrated as a social event, with friends dropping in to offer encouragement, bear witness, record the delivery, tweet about it, and post it on Facebook. The conver-sation is no longer limited to how well the new mother is doing, but extends to how well she did. Back in the bedroom, Big Pharma awaits with its billion-dollar line of products for boosting sexual performance. Regardless of whether the anxiety strikes in the penis or at the piano, the same rule applies: You have to be in control of your instrument.

Many performers eschew the subject. Studies have shown that up to 30 percent of orchestra musicians rely on beta-blockers to slow their autonomic nervous systems prior to a performance. Many of them willingly share their prescription stashes with their colleagues, but few care to delve into the problem that precipitates it. "It's such a touchy topic," a young pianist in New York told me, practically recoiling. "It seems like it would be bad luck to talk about it." The American psychiatrist Glen Gabbard wrote about "an unspoken conspiracy of silence" among musicians and other performers about stage fright.[6] Before a performance, he noted, "the experience of stage fright is seldom alluded to, as if the mere mention of it will cause the reaction to intensify." It's been said that every pianist's anxiety is as unique as his or her fingerprints. One detects an almost existential dread of contamination, as if stage fright were as transmittable as a virus on a doorknob.

And maybe they're right to steer clear. Though anxiety contagion can't be traced as systemically as bird flu, it shares some of the same qualities. That much was demonstrated in the spring of 2012, when a succession of Tourette-like cases ran through the small western New York town of Le Roy. A cluster of high school girls, many of them cheerleaders, had begun to exhibit uncontrolled tics, twitches, stutters, and jerks. It happened at the dinner table and in the classroom. TV news cameras raced to record the girls, their arms lurching, heads yanking, legs tottering like zombies in a B movie. Two cases jumped to eighteen, and parents grew convinced that there had been an undisclosed environmental disaster. Erin Brockovich, the environmental activist, was called in to investigate. In the end, the girls were diagnosed with a condition called "conversion disorder," a mass psychogenic illness better known as mass hysteria. The neurologists who treated them concluded that they were subconsciously converting stress into physical symptoms.

As it happens, cases of mass hysteria have more than once involved cheerleaders. In a *New York Times Magazine* story about the Le Roy case, reporter Susan Dominus suggested that it was the girls' organizational unity that made them susceptible to influence.[7] She cited a 2002 incident in which ten students, five of them cheerleaders, from a rural town in North Carolina suffered nonepileptic seizures and fainting spells. In 1952, 165 members of a cheerleading squad in Monroe, Louisiana, fainted before halftime at a high school football game. Five ambulances raced across the field to attend to the stricken girls. "It looked like the racetrack at Indianapolis," a spectator told the Associated Press. In Le Roy, doctors advised parents and school administrators to stop talking about it so publicly. The media attention was halted, and after a few months, the girls improved markedly, mostly after learning relaxation techniques and, in some cases, taking anxiety medication.

Stage fright exposes the foolishness of the body, so easily deceived and outmaneuvered by the mind. Naturally, people are loath to accept it. How can symptoms so excessive and seemingly life-threatening proceed from mere anxiety? The British actor Michael Gambon, the lovable Dumbledore in the Harry Potter films, has twice been rushed to the hospital for symptoms of stage fright. In 2013, his performance anxiety forced him to withdraw from a play at the National Theatre in London.[8] The American evangelist Rick Warren, minister of the twenty-two-thousand-member Saddleback Church in Southern California, has explained his public-speaking problem as a purely physiological brain malfunction, though most neuroscientists would call it stage fright. His symptoms are so extreme that they have temporarily blinded him: "When I stand up to speak and adrenaline hits my system, I cannot see until that adrenaline drains out. It is a very rare disorder; I have been to all the top clinics in the world, and they said they may name a syndrome after me! There are only fourteen or fifteen people they know of who have it. It makes public speaking excruciatingly painful. Everyone knows that adrenaline is a public speaker's best friend: If you do not have adrenaline, you are boring. You need it for passion. So when I get up to speak, adrenaline hits my system like any public speaker. I am not talking about nerves; I speak to 22,000 people every Sunday morning. I am not talking about stage fright. I have spoken in the Superdome three times. I have spoken to over a million people at one time. But when adrenaline hits my system, I go almost blind until it drains out. When I got up here, you did not know it, but I could not see you. I could not even see my notes."[9]

A syndrome *was* named after Steve Blass, the Pittsburgh Pirates pitcher who woke up one day in 1973 to discover he could no longer find the strike zone. He had been among the dominant pitchers in the major leagues, with a ninety-mile-per-hour fastball and a nearly unhittable slider. The latter pitch was notoriously hard to control, but Blass was so sure of himself that he'd throw it even when behind in the count. He won eighteen games for the Pirates in 1968 and another sixteen in 1969. He was a member of the National League All-Star team in 1972 and finished second in that year's voting for the Cy Young Award. When he collapsed, when "the Thing" brought him to his knees, it was like a real-life version of *Groundhog Day*: Inning after inning, as if in a dream, he walked batters, threw wild pitches straight to the backstop, and allowed a multitude of stolen bases. The most mystifying thing about it was that when he threw alone with a catcher in the bullpen, he was as good as ever.

Blass consulted psychologists, tried transcendental meditation, and ran down every tip, no matter how patently ridiculous, including, famously, one fan's suggestion that he invest in a loose set of boxers. Forty years later, I phoned him at his home in Pennsylvania. A good-natured man who had spent the intervening decades as a Pirates TV color commentator, he didn't mind talking about it. "Steve Blass disease" had become part of the baseball lexicon. He understood the fascination: "It's so damn illusive unless you're living it." And though he never could figure out why it struck him in the first place, he all too clearly understood the physiology. "I would physically tighten up—and you can't pitch like that. No flow, you're just hoping the ball will go where you want it to, but you don't expect it to."

Tightening up is the key, as etymology bears out. The word *anxiety* comes from the Old French *anguere*, meaning to choke, constrict, strangle, or cut off at the airway. It describes the very hallmark of performance anxiety—the rapid, shallow breathing that occurs when the muscles contract and you begin to shake. Utterance of the word forces the tongue backward, blocking off the throat. In other words, just saying the word embodies its very meaning. The harder you try to control these muscles, the more they tremble. So we choke, bite the apple, and gasp for breath.

Google "stage fright" and you get more than seven million hits—a catalog of phobias, instant cures, and celebrities who wrestle with their anxiety. For some, it comes and goes like malaria, showing up at the most unexpected times. Laurence Olivier was fifty-seven, long regarded as the world's foremost actor, when he suddenly became crippled by stage fright while playing Othello. It never subsided, and for the next ten years of his career, he had to be pushed onstage, where his fellow actors were forbidden to look him in the eye. Mahatma Gandhi was only a young lawyer in England when he attended a small gathering of a vegetarian society, stood to read a few remarks, and discovered that he could not speak: "My vision became blurred and I trembled, though the speech hardly covered a sheet of foolscap." Thomas Jefferson's law career was disrupted by a fear of public speaking. His voice would "sink in his throat" whenever he tried to give a speech, according to one biographer. In his eight years as president, Jefferson delivered only two—the inaugural address for his first and second terms.

When, in March 2012, U.S. solicitor general Donald Verrilli went before the Supreme Court in defense of President Barack Obama's health care legislation, he was a player at the highest level of his profession, a lawyer who had argued more than a hundred high court cases. But this one became a train wreck. At the beginning of his oral argument, he stumbled and stammered. When he paused to sip from a glass of water, the ice cubes clinked louder than his words. He lost his place, repeated himself, his voice quivering as he asked the justices to excuse him. A blogger from *Mother Jones* compared his performance with that of a teenager giving a high school oral presentation for the first time and opined that Verrilli should be grateful the Supreme Court didn't allow cameras in the courtroom. Another publication derided him as "a case of stage fright that skipped right past funny and went directly to pitiable." If Obamacare went down, as so many prematurely predicted, it would be the fault of Verrilli's "pathetic" performance.

According to one theory, stage fright is a phenomenon of modernity. Nicholas Ridout, a British cultural theorist, dates it to the introduction in 1879 of electric lights in theaters across England and Europe. Prior to that time, auditoriums were never completely darkened; now, with a flick of a switch, a hall could be blackened, leaving the performer isolated in the spotlight, staring out at an invisible void. The theaters of ancient Greece had been outdoor affairs, designed to take advantage of sunlight, while those of the Renaissance depended on oil lamps, torches, and candles. A painting from 1670 of the Comédie-Française in Paris shows a stage lit by six chandeliers and a bank of thirty-four "footlights," large candles requiring a crew of candlesnuffers to extinguish. By the eighteenth century, the Drury Lane Theatre in London had introduced a "float," a long metal trough filled with oil, in which metal saucers, each holding a flickering wick, would bob like buoys. The trough was lowered into a hatch in the stage floor by ropes and pulleys, to create a dimming effect.

The inception of gas lighting in the early nineteenth century allowed for still greater control. Now, a near blackout could be achieved. But theater operators weren't interested in darkness: They understood that the ruling classes went to the theater to see and be seen, to flirt and conduct business, to show off their costumes and jewels. In nineteenth-century novels, from

Madame Bovary to *The Mill on the Floss* and *War and Peace*, the opera glass is turned on the audience more frequently—and to greater plot effect—than on the stage. The opening scene of Edith Wharton's *The Age of Innocence* (published in 1920) is a classic case. When Newland Archer trains his opera glass on his fiancée's box, he catches sight of another woman—the tempting princess Ellen Olenska, "with brown hair growing in close curls about her temples and held in place by a narrow band of diamonds." So much for the opera.

The social role of the theater demanded a brightly lit auditorium. But composer Richard Wagner and other radicals of the second half of the nineteenth century were pushing a different agenda. Wagner's Bayreuth audiences sat in utter darkness, eager to merge with the composer's metaphysical epics—with his *Gesamtkunstwerk*, the grand unification of the arts. The theater gradually was becoming less a social setting than a quasi-mystical one, no small thanks to the power of electricity.

In his book *Stage Fright, Animals, and Other Theatrical Problems*, Ridout says that the introduction of electricity in 1879 coincided with these changing ideas about the role of theater and paved the way for a major shift in the balance of power between performers and their audiences. Now the center of attention belonged more fully to the actor and musician, whose social roles were simultaneously undergoing major changes. No longer retained by the court, they were becoming independent contractors and thus newly vulnerable to the economic approval of the modern-day audience or "entertainment consumer." The approval of that audience had a direct impact on the performer's very employment and economic success.

These changes further coincided with a new paradigm of acting then coming to prominence and making unprecedented demands on performers. The Stanislavski system, developed in the late nineteenth century by the Russian actor and director Constantin Stanislavski, required that actors go deep into their own psyches for "emotion memory," to make their most intimate experiences the basis of their performances. "It is not just the actor's professional credibility or employment prospects that are at stake when he or she steps on stage," writes Ridout, "it is his or her self: a negative response from an audience is no longer just a comment on professional accomplishment, it has become a judgement upon the inner self. This judgement is exercised in darkness. The actor under scrutiny is initially blinded by the light, and even when this effect fades as the eyes adjust, the auditorium presents an undifferentiated darkness."[10]

Stanislavski chronicled his own stage fright in *An Actor Prepares*, a barely fictionalized account of his younger self— the aspiring actor Kostya, who one day steps to the front of the stage and peers out into "the awful hole" as he performs the role of Othello (the same role, incidentally, that precipitated Olivier's stage fright).[11] It is only a rehearsal, but his terror grows, so that by the time of performance, "the fear and attraction of the public seemed stronger than ever" and Kostya is paralyzed. His voice makes high-pitched sounds, his hands have turned to stone, and he can barely breathe. He feels severed from the world. And then, as he gasps the famous

line "Blood, Iago, blood!" a murmur runs through the audience, signaling some deep-seated recognition. Somehow, the
feelings of terror and rage against his own helplessness—and
his stage fright—have created something real. Ridout suggests
the "awful hole" could serve as a stand-in for Kostya's very
soul. It could also symbolize the vagina, he adds, then immediately cautions the reader not to put too much stock in this
Freudian suggestion. "It would be wrong to suggest that
every, or indeed, any actor experiencing stage fright is reliv-
ing some infant anxiety about origins, membranes and fluids."
Sometimes a cigar is just a cigar.

The act of getting up onstage is, by its nature, an aggressive
act: "Look at me! Listen to me!" the performer demands,
whether it's to speak, act, play music, preach or argue before a
court of law. When the performance is deemed a failure, the
audience may consider itself entitled to lash back—Hiss! Boo!
Splat go the tomatoes. The actor or musician must wrest
control of the crowd, like a lion tamer whipping the beast into
submission. Stephen Aaron, a New York psychologist, actor,
and director, writes about this mutual antagonism in *Stage
Fright: Its Role in Acting*: "The audience remains the bad presence in the house—the uninvited—threatening to persecute
the actor by humiliation, ridicule, starvation, and indifference
until the actor has made contact with them, until the stage
and the house are merged."[12] Aaron duly notes that performance is an aggressive/erotic endeavor, never more apparent
than in the confrontational language unique to backstage
theater: "Knock 'em dead," "Fuck 'em," "Lay 'em in the
aisles." Olivier used to stand behind the curtain, muttering

"You bastards" at his audience. Blythe Danner buoyed her spirits with the battle cry "Go out there and maim them."

As a child actor on the New York stage, Eric Brown knew nothing of such one-way confrontations; he exhibited a panache that made older actors envious. He began his career at four, blowing bubbles through a straw in a Listerine commercial. When he was twelve, he played Pippin in the musical's national touring cast. At thirteen, he made his Broadway debut in *On Golden Pond*. Two years later, he was cast as Phillip Fillmore in the 1981 film *Private Lessons*, a steamy coming-of-age comedy about a teenager seduced by his thirty-something French governess. The Dutch actress Sylvia Kristel, star of the soft-porn *Emmanuelle* films, played the sexy governess, and *Private Lessons* became a cult sensation. Brown was golden. After graduating high school, he took off for Los Angeles to join the cast of *Mama's Family*, a spin-off of *The Carol Burnett Show*.

But he soon found himself adrift. On the first day of shooting, when cued to introduce his character on camera, he opened his mouth and said, "Ah . . ." He tried again. "My name is . . ." He couldn't remember his character's name, and it took three takes before he could say his line: "My name is Buzz!" That mishap set in motion a pattern of anxiety attacks that undermined his confidence and derailed his career. Cast in a two-character play titled *Mass Appeal*, Brown and his stage partner stumbled on opening night, repeating three pages of dialogue three times.

"And everybody knew it. It was like watching an animal on *Animal Kingdom* that isn't dead yet." Though he's telling it from a distance of thirty years, he winces as he recounts the experience. He broke out in hives and developed gastrointestinal problems. His doctor advised him to quit acting before he made himself sick. And then came the final blow. *Mama's Family*—Brown was still in the cast—was canceled. "I had just come off a movie that made a lot of money. I had a big-shot agent. Then he dropped me, which was devastating. I felt I had underachieved, I felt I had underperformed."

Brown enrolled at the University of California at Berkeley and majored in political science. He worked as press secretary to a New York congresswoman and eventually returned to California as communications director for the William and Flora Hewlett Foundation, where today he trains his staff how to be effective public speakers. The most important thing, he tells them, is plenty of practice. He can see in an instant when someone is nervous. Men tap their feet; their voices go dry. Women's necks bloom shades of red and purple; their voices turn squeaky and thin. People develop telltale idiosyncrasies. Whenever one of his colleagues is called upon to speak, she picks up her ever-present can of Diet Coke, then sets it down, picks it up, and sets it down, obsessively, without ever taking a sip. Brown has recommended that she leave the drink back at her desk.

Yet, ironically, he still gets what he calls "a modified version of stage fright," rambling and losing focus when it's his turn to perform. He procrastinates when the next presentation looms, because, frankly, he would rather not think about it. "The high irony is that I train people to give presentations and make sure they practice like crazy."

Chapter 3

TOUCHING A TARANTULA

I RETURNED TO THE piano when I was forty-nine, prodded by my youngest son, Jesse, who had just discovered jazz. I had occasionally accompanied the other boys—Ben on flute and Max on violin—until each surpassed my sight-reading skills. It had been one of my favorite things to do with them when they were little, as long as no one was sitting and listening in judgment. But Jesse was demanding something more. He wanted me to improvise along with him on the clarinet, and he refused to accept my protestations that I had no knowledge of jazz and no idea where to begin. Finally, after months of prodding, I called an acquaintance whom I knew to be a fine pianist, someone who played both jazz and classical, to get some pointers.

Because it had been so long—thirty years—since I had sat down and actually practiced, Landis Gwynn suggested I brush up with some classical music for a couple of weeks. It would help get my hands back into shape. I went back to the Mozart Sonata in A Minor, the one I had first played for Mr. Weiss, and the *Bagatelles* by Alexander Tcherepnin, which my aunty

Maddy had played for me when I was a toddler lying under her piano. I started picking my way through a Brahms inter- mezzo, a Bach prelude and fugue, and the first movement of Beethoven's *Waldstein* Sonata.

At my first lesson, I was so nervous that I could hardly play through a line without a blunder. My hands shook. I apolo- gized almost nonstop. "My God, Sara, what did they do to you?" Landis demanded. I took lessons with him for six years and never did move on to jazz. He taught me how to practice in new ways, to take apart seemingly impossible passages and deconstruct them in various rhythms. I was his only student— he made his living as a tech writer—but he prepared for our lessons with a commitment that matched my own. He listened to multiple recordings of whatever piece I was working on at the time, scrutinized the score, and sight-read it through before coming to our weekly lesson with specific ideas about how I should approach the music.

Landis was a burly man who had played offensive tackle on his Connecticut high school's undefeated football team, and even in his fifties he had a robust metabolism. He sweated profusely during our lessons, and it became a custom for him to laughingly excuse himself, usually around the halfway point, to wash up and change his shirt. We were unprepared for how serious and important these lessons would become to us both. By now, I was practicing two or three hours in the evenings, tackling increasingly difficult music, and surprising myself and my teacher with my appetite for work.

I sometimes wondered if I was like Ivan Ilyich, the Tolstoy character who recognizes in his last days that he has lived all

Landis Gwynn (Marilyn Gwynn)

wrong, that he didn't get what life was about until it was too late. I practiced with a seriousness and dedication that I had never had when I was young, which made me ask myself why I hadn't stuck with it. Was it because I was lazy or because I didn't understand what was actually required to be good at something? As I began deconstructing difficult passages, breaking them down—hands apart, practicing whole measures in syncopated rhythms, closing my eyes to get the feel of the music in my body, sometimes running the same measures a dozen times, sometimes a hundred—I admitted to myself that I was, in important ways, learning to play for the first time in my life.

But still I refused to play for an audience, and whenever Landis suggested the idea, I quoted my childhood hero, Glenn Gould, who said that his ideal artist-to-audience ratio was one to zero. I found myself gravitating to the surreptitious performance, best executed with the listener as fly on the wall. For this to work, the person had to overhear me playing in the background, either on the phone or from the sidewalk outside my front door. Sure enough, I began to meet people in the neighborhood who told me they occasionally stood outside and listened to me play.

My favorite such instance occurred soon after Rich and I inherited a little house on Lake Champlain in upstate New York. We began flying back east every summer to spend a month on the lake, hike in the Adirondacks, and see old friends. The only drawback was that the house, an 1839 clapboard colonial, didn't come with a piano. It wasn't long, however, before I met Ethel Bernard, the ninety-something widow of a former violist of the Boston Symphony Orchestra and herself an excellent pianist.

Bernard kept a beautiful Yamaha grand piano in her barn a few blocks from our house, and every winter she had it moved into storage, to be returned to her cool, uninsulated barn when the weather grew warm. Years earlier, when she was in her eighties, she'd given concerts in the barn for which an overflow crowd gathered on folding chairs and blankets on the lawn outside. She invited me to play her piano whenever I wanted; the barn door was always open. She herself rarely played anymore, though she was so vigorous that when I walked over to her place one afternoon to take her up on her offer, I came upon her in the middle of building a stone wall.

I loved playing that piano, though the light inside the barn was bad and the air was hot and humid. These conditions required that I leave the barn door ajar, which let the music drift out and make its way up to the covered porch where Bernard often sat and—apparently—listened. I was once informed that she told her neighbors I was "a very fine pianist." That was gratifying, but mostly I appreciated that she never entered the barn.

Back in California, Landis was less decorous. In 2011, after years of weekly lessons, he announced that the time had come for me to give a little recital. "Little" was the operative word: The invited guests included Jesse, my only child still living at home, Rich, Landis, and his wife, Marilyn. Since Marilyn couldn't make it, that left three people on the sofa. By the time I got to the second page of the prelude from Debussy's *Suite Bergamasque*, I was a mess. I botched one easy run after another until, finally, I gave up in disgust and flung the music on the floor. "Damn it, Landis," I snapped. "You knew I didn't want to do this. It's all your fault."

My little audience urged me to resume, and eventually I did, gathering up the score and taking the piece from the beginning to the final chords. All proclaimed it a great success. But when Landis left the house, I felt suddenly mortified. Nobody talked about what had happened, but it hung in the air along with the inexorable questions: How meaningful was it to study and practice so diligently if I was unwilling or unable to share the music? Was it worth all this effort just to play for myself?

I posed these questions in an emotional phone call to one of my oldest friends, who declared that it was high time I faced my demons. Amy Linn had been hearing my stories for years; all her entreaties to hear me play had been swiftly denied. Now, at her instigation, I signed up for a group piano class at my local community college. It was a nurturing atmosphere, held in a classroom filled with forty electronic keyboards, twelve of which were occupied by students of widely varying talents and abilities. There were two grand pianos at the front of the room, and when the teacher called on me one night, I walked up confidently, set my hands on the keyboard, and ran my fingers up the first broken chord. As they lifted off the keys, I saw that they were shaking like hummingbirds at a feeder. All these years later and my leap to panic still came as the ultimate betrayal. *Et tu, Brute?*

It was as if my body were hardwired, back in some deep, cellular pit to which I had no access. I kept playing, but my hands were shaking so uncontrollably that I could hardly strike the chords. I gazed down at myself from a distance high above the keys, watching a body that was no longer in charge. My fear was at the controls, like an independent organism emerging from inside me, my own Rosemary's baby. Soon, I was paying more attention to the shakes than the music, and though I managed to make it to the end, it was with an embarrassing array of hiccups and gaffes. Driving home in the dark, feeling depressed and angry, thirsting for a big glass of wine, I asked myself for the thousandth time if I was just one of those people who shouldn't perform. Julie Jaffee Nagel, an Ann Arbor psychoanalyst, had intimated as much when I called her up for some advice. A pianist who graduated with two degrees in performance from Juilliard, Nagel was, I took it, speaking from personal experience. "I see it as the symptom of a constellation of problems," she said. "There are some people who should not perform. You see them self-sabotaging all the time." For individuals like us, she seemed to imply, the act of performance was an act against gravity.

Many of my favorite performers had improvised strategies to tame their demons. Brilliantly, pianist Sviatoslav Richter had settled his nerves by turning the house lights on the audience and off himself, save for a reading light above his musical score. He said this freed the listener "to concentrate on the music rather than on the performer." In a *New Yorker* piece about the terrors of stage fright, the drama critic John Lahr described Richter's decision as one that conjured "an illusion of invisibility" for the pianist.[1] Lahr interviewed Carly Simon, who is almost as famous for her stage fright as for her singing. She, too, has turned the lights on the audience and then gone far beyond that innocent trick. Backstage before performances, she has jabbed herself with safety pins and persuaded her band members to spank her. "Simon has found that physical pain often trumps psychological terror," Lahr wrote.

Arthur Golden recounted something similar in his novel *Memoirs of a Geisha*, which was loosely based on the life of a retired geisha in Japan. The book's protagonist, Chiyo Sakamoto, describes how she was made to plunge her hands into icy water before carrying her shakuhachi and koto, traditional Japanese instruments, out into the snow, wind, and rain to practice. "I know it sounds terribly cruel, but it's the way things were done back then," she explains matter-of-factly. "And in fact, toughening the hands in this way really did help me play better. You see, stage fright drains the feeling from your hands; and when you've already grown accustomed to playing with hands that are numbed and miserable, stage fright presents much less of a problem."[2]

It reminded me of a recital I once attended by pianist Charles Rosen in San Jose, California. He was performing the three late Beethoven sonatas, and you could feel the excitement in the hall as the hour approached. But there were parking complications and the concert was briefly delayed. It began twenty minutes later than scheduled, and Rosen played as if he were making up for lost time. Jaw clenched, he attacked the music percussively, angrily, while missing notes, many of them. It was an unhappy performance by a renowned musician and musicologist, whose analytic texts of classical composers are part of the twentieth century's critical canon. After intermission, as more than a few elderly people inched their way down the aisle to their seats, Rosen strode back onstage, glanced at the dawdlers, and plunged into the music: Sonata no. 32 in C Minor, op. 111, Beethoven's farewell piano sonata. His glance carried disdain, but perhaps also a fear of the audience writ large, as he himself once acknowledged in an essay: "The popular idol is greeted as he enters with acclaim by the audience because he is, for its sake, about to expose himself to the danger of public humiliation. At any moment the singer's voice may crack on a high note, the pianist fall off his stool, the violinist drop his instrument, the conductor give a disastrous cue and irretrievably confuse the orchestra. The applause that rewards the performer who has come through unscathed is tinged with regret."[3] Rosen's own fears seemed to rise to a crescendo with this sentence: "The silence of the audience is not that of a public that listens but of one that watches—like the dead hush that accompanies the unsteady movement of the tightrope walker poised over his perilous space."

How true. Seated at the piano, attempting to play some vast piece from memory, without a score, one might as well be perched on the high wire without a net. The thin margin of safety depends on absolute precision. Every note, every step, carries a search for balance over a fixed point on the wire. The analogy of the tightrope is one so often raised by classical musicians that I wondered what a real tightrope walker would say about it.

I found Pete Sweet, a circus artist originally from Berkeley, California, studying at a school for clowns in Florence, Italy. We spoke a few times over Skype—long, rambling conversations following his long days of juggling and slack-rope walking. Then thirty-nine, Sweet had learned to juggle while a student at Berkeley High. His parents were free-minded religious scholars, ex-hippies who took their three kids out of school to travel the world for a year, then settled for a time in central Java to start a school. It was in Indonesia, when he was seventeen, where Sweet first tied a rope between a coconut tree and the porch of his father's house and teetered across. He went on to study Indonesian at the University of Wisconsin, playing in a gamelan, a traditional Indonesian orchestra, and practicing his juggling. He had walked the tight wire several years before discovering the slack rope. It offered up a whole other challenge. As its name states, the tightrope is taut and relatively stationary, while the slack rope is always moving, undulating beneath one's feet. "Of course the center is always in yourself, but on the tightrope you keep your center *above* the wire," Sweet explained. In other words, your center stays fixed. But in slack, your center—that balance point—is elusive: "In slack, you move the rope *underneath* you. It's like being able to move the ground. It's moving, but you also move, so in some way you're influencing and controlling it, and in other ways it's influencing you; you're not at all in control." It sounded like playing the piano.

Falling off the tightrope is like falling off a log, he continued, while falling off the slack rope is like having a carpet pulled out from under you: "My teacher says that falling is like death. It's something we all know is going to happen; we just don't know how it's going to happen." Over the years, Sweet has walked tightropes and slack ropes in troupes across Europe; he was part of a vaudeville-style circus act, singing and dancing for thousands of spectators. But it wasn't until he attended a workshop in Paris, where he was challenged to imagine himself on the high wire—while still very much grounded on terra firma—that Sweet experienced his first and only panic attack. The experience shocked him; until that moment, he hadn't realized how afraid he actually felt. "I read an article by a big wave surfer who said that nobody's fearless when they surf big waves unless they're certifiably insane. You can't be fearless out there, you can only be panicless. I think I had maintained my own poise for years by being numb to my

fear. The fact that I was continually putting myself in scary .
situations and asking myself that I be poised and not
panicked—it was much easier to do that without being aware
of my fear," he said. The panic experience at the workshop
inspired his next show: a performance of Maximilian, a clown
with a bad case of stage fright walking the slack rope.

Sweet quoted Fritz Perls, the German-born founder of
Gestalt therapy, who defined fear as excitement without
breath. When we're in a state of fear and panic, our breath gets
shallow. Our abdomen fills with butterflies because normal
digestion shuts down. The tension causes numbness. Our
body retracts; we numb the fear. The most important thing
Sweet learned was breathing—whether he was walking the
slack rope up in the air or walking on his hands on solid
ground. Breathing—so autonomic, so much a function of the
reptilian brain—is so easy to forget.

"Part of the training has been to focus on the technique
and hone it so it's precise," Sweet said. "With every step, I first
touch the side of the rope with my foot. Then I transfer my
weight onto the foot, setting it on the rope, which is moving
all the time. And that's what I do with each step: First I feel
the side of the rope—like the side of a pencil. It becomes so
innate you do it very quickly. That's something I focus on, but
once I do that, I will intentionally distract myself and look
from side to side, do things with my hand."

I'd been half listening to this discourse on the mechanics of
slack-rope footwork, when I suddenly recognized the similar-
ity to what I was learning at the piano. As I practiced my
scales and arpeggios each day, I often tried to distract myself,

to move my head from side to side and up and down, as a way of freeing myself from the very precision I was working so hard to achieve. We were in parallel worlds, Pete Sweet on his slack rope, I at my piano—both of us searching for the place where fear evaporates long enough for freedom and joy to reach the surface.

Sweet was a classic autodidact whose years of study in juggling, dance, clowning, mime, and breath work amounted to a self-directed Ph.D. program. Listening to him, it became apparent that I had to design my own course of action, one requiring that I undergo the kind of exposure therapy with which claustrophobics, arachnophobics, and other neurotics typically are treated. I had heard reports of claustrophobics shut away in car trunks and coffins by their therapists, of arachnophobics cajoled into playing with tarantulas.

The equivalent for me was to confront an audience. So without allowing myself too much time to think about it, I went ahead and scheduled a solo recital for June 30, 2013, the day before my sixtieth birthday. It was now early June 2012. That left me just over a year to prepare, to "expose" myself; I imagined it as a round of inoculations, a series of graduated steps. As the year progressed, they would serve as my road map. In the first few months, I would perform in retirement homes and hospitals. I would attend a nine-day piano camp in Bennington, Vermont, sign up for master classes at which I would play before other piano students and be critiqued by a teacher. I would routinely drop by the closest major airport to perform on a piano that sat, invitingly, just outside of the baggage claim area. In the last few months of my campaign—

my year of living dangerously—I would organize a series of informal evening "soirees," inviting small groups of friends and acquaintances to my house for music and wine. My teacher would arrange for me to play before several top pianists in the San Francisco Bay Area. Then, in May 2013, I would perform a half-hour solo recital at the local public library. After all that, I told myself, I would be ready to play before fifty or more invited guests in a public hall—my grand performance. But first, I had to touch a few tarantulas.

Chapter 4

ARE YOU MY GURU?

My CONCERT WAS STILL nearly a year away, but the thought of it was already disturbing my dreams, reigning over my nights, plunging me deep into Emily Dickinson country, where, as she said, you don't have to be a house to be haunted. I felt haunted, wondering at my own recklessness. Why was I doing this to myself? Was it too late to change my mind? How was I ever going to pull it off? When I did sleep, my dreams were piano possessed. In one, I laid my fingers on the keyboard and then couldn't pry them off. They were superglued to the keys. In another dream, I looked down at my belly, saw that I was pregnant, and opened my mouth just as two small hands fluttered out of it, waving delicately in the air before my eyes. They were just a baby's hands, I noted, but the fingers were long and graceful and I congratulated myself on the fact that this child of mine was going to be born with piano hands.

Some of my apprehension stemmed from the fact that I found myself without a teacher. I had an almost religious belief in the power of a great teacher. Throughout my life, I'd been inspired by numerous teachers and in recent years had seen what the right ones could accomplish with my sons. One in particular stood out. Mary Lou Galen became my son's violin teacher soon after he entered high school. Max was innately musical, but stubborn and resistant to instruction. His previous teacher couldn't get through to him; he had developed a way of looking through her and closing his ears to almost everything she said. When Galen took him on, she did so on the condition that I sit through the lessons and take notes. I was taken aback; I had always spent the kids' lesson times running errands, meeting friends for coffee, making a deadline, or catching up on my reading. Now, in addition to all my other responsibilities, I was being asked to take on the job of stenographer.

It didn't take long for me to realize that I'd been admitted into what amounted to an exclusive lecture series, a year's worth of master classes with a master teacher. Galen, a former concertmaster with the San Jose Symphony Orchestra, had suffered repetitive stress injury and no longer played the violin. Unable to demonstrate technique, tone, or style, she had learned to communicate by using story and metaphor.

As a young violinist, she had been mentored by Raphael Bronstein ("Mr. Bronstein," as she always referred to him), a Russian pedagogue who taught at the Manhattan School of Music in New York. She kept his framed photograph—bald head, eagle nose—on prominent display in her studio and quoted him at least once every lesson. Trained in the Russian School, a style of virtuoso violin technique that's been passed down for more than 150 years, Galen demanded precision as well as a rich, warm tone. She could not abide anything less than perfect intonation; in every orchestra she ever played in, she said, there were seasoned violinists who played out of tune. It drove her crazy. During the first few months of Max's lessons, she devoted each entire session to a single scale, working it note by note, assiduously, so slowly that the hour typically ran out before Max made it back down to the bottom. To my astonishment, he accepted her constant, grueling critiques. At home, he started keeping a practice log and I could hear him after school, practicing behind his bedroom door with a new discipline inspired by her counsel: "When you practice, you're a cold-blooded scientist. When you perform, you play for yourself and for God."

My youngest son had a different relationship to music. At thirteen, Jesse was becoming passionate about jazz; his great ambition was to be the next Benny Goodman. He had started off on the clarinet a few years earlier and was now begging us to buy him a tenor saxophone, presumably so he could become the next John Coltrane. We didn't take him very seriously. He was a boy of serial obsessions who from the age of seven had moved from baseball to dirt bike riding, tae kwon do, and karate. When he was nine, he began spending three hours a day, six days a week, at the neighborhood dojo, working out with teenagers and adults, plotting his path to the Olympics. He talked me into joining him there, and after months of resistance I found myself throwing punches and kicks, urged on by a traditional Korean instructor. Master Song gave long lectures, during which he admonished the few women in the class to replace our natural proclivity for gossip with kicking.

"Yes, sir!" the students shouted at his every pause. He promised that tae kwon do would immunize us against breast
cancer and other maladies if we would just learn to breathe
deeply. In one lecture, he assured us that criminals were all,
without exception, shallow breathers. If one were to conduct
a study of inmates at San Quentin or any other prison, he
asserted, one would find a population of shallow breathers.
Did he really say that? we'd later demand on our way out the
door. Still, he was a formidable teacher and a ninth-degree
black belt. The men in the class revered him; the women
occasionally rolled their eyes but respected him. He could put
his finger on every student's weakness and call him on it
before a roomful of spectators. He once told me, during a test
for a new color belt, that I allowed my emotions to get in the
way of whatever I sought to accomplish. It was humiliating. It
was true.

One day, after dragging me to the dojo for two years, Jesse
announced that the Olympics no longer played a part in his
foreseeable future. He was going to be a musician and I was to
be his accompanist—at least until he could find someone else.
The year was 2002, and once again my protestations fell flat.
Jesse by now was going on thirteen, and I realized that his
desire to involve me in his life would soon come to an end.
After a few months of delay, I replaced Master Song with
Landis Gwynn, my piano-playing, tech-writer acquaintance.

Landis had grown up in a Connecticut suburb, the son of
an English professor who had been one of the foremost experts
on William Faulkner. He began taking piano lessons when he
was six years old and showed an early affinity for music. He

adored his teacher, Doris Lehnert, a vivacious young woman who was "the real deal": small, but with large, powerful hands and a ferocious technique. At the age of eleven, he performed with a local orchestra, playing the slow movement of Mozart's Piano Concerto no. 23 in A Major. It appeared that he was headed for a life in music.

But when he was thirteen, catastrophe struck. It happened during a ski trip to Killington, Vermont. Just a moment after passing his father on the slopes, a skier caught up with him and told him that his dad was in trouble up the mountain. The boy herringboned it back up and found his father lying face-up in the snow with a stranger bent over him, giving mouth-to-mouth resuscitation. A small helicopter whirred down and his father was rushed inside and flown away, declared dead before the chopper touched down at the nearest hospital. He was forty-nine and the cause of death was heart attack.

As Landis recalled, there was never any discussion at home, just a tacit understanding that he would no longer play the piano. "No one knew what to do except, well, piano playing is supposed to be fun, but we were sad now. So we were not going to do that." Landis didn't touch the piano for the next five years. He made his way back to it as a freshman at the University of Pennsylvania, where, miserable and for the first time overwhelmed by the enormity of his aloneness, he signed up for a music class and began recognizing snippets of symphonies and concertos, music he hadn't heard in years. One afternoon, as he was listening, he recalled as in a dream that he too used to play the piano. He found a practice room in the music department, borrowed a few scores from the library, and relearned how to read music. He began studying in earnest, immersing himself in a life that had been snatched away from him.

Though he didn't pursue the piano upon graduation, Landis was someone who listened and analyzed with the ear and erudition of a scholar. He knew practically every note in all thirty-two Beethoven piano sonatas and could sing any one of the movements at random. We went to concerts together, met in coffee shops to hash over our lives, shared dinner with each other's families. And as we became friends, I sometimes took advantage of his gentle demeanor. He once suggested that I learn a Brahms romanze, a piece ripe with the dense chords characteristic of the composer. It would, he suggested, be a good way to work on voicing, meaning the task of articulating specific notes within chords as a way of advancing the melodic line. I worked on the first page happily. But as soon as I began reading over the second section, I became flustered by a series of huge leaps that had to be played pianissimo, at softest volume. How could I possibly manage with these small hands, I objected, and tossed the music aside. When Landis laughed nervously in protest and acquiesced, I sensed the end of a chapter: I needed someone who would push me, someone I couldn't push around. I needed a new teacher.

I had recently become friendly with Mark Rothman (name changed at his request), a bear of a man with stout fingers that at first glance didn't look as if they were designed for the piano. He was a transplanted New Yorker who loved music, food, and books—probably in that order. We met after he began playing music with my son Max, and I felt an instant

camaraderie with him. After I became his student, I appreciated the way he talked about music. Don't be coy, he once
cautioned me on the way I ended a partita—applying the
language and sensibility of Jane Austen to Johann Sebastian
Bach. He had an affinity for Bach, and so did I. As we experimented with different articulations (legato versus detached)
and debated the merits and drawbacks of pedaling, the hour-
long lessons flew by.

The last couple of years had been difficult for Rothman.
The economy had taken a toll after the 2008 stock market
crash, and he more than once confided his frustration that he,
a pianist with impressive friends in the classical world, was
now teaching children to read music. He himself had studied
with a series of strong-minded teachers, the most memorable
being "a Svengali" nicknamed "Sadie." As boys, he and his
older brother took three buses to her apartment at the other
end of Brooklyn for Saturday lessons in clarinet, bassoon, and
piano. They arrived early in the morning and returned home
to their own flat well after midnight—having babysat Sadie's
children, gazed at the Impressionist prints on her walls, and
gorged themselves on her imported cheeses. It was a different
world from the working-class one they knew, and they
worshipped her. It was years before either realized that their
teacher lacked all interest in or knowledge of piano technique,
so that by the time they reached high school they had acquired
serious deficiencies.

Rothman began slinking away for lessons at the Mannes
College in Manhattan, then to a professor at Queens College.
When he finally 'fessed up and told Sadie that he wanted to

change teachers, she exiled him from her studio. A few years later, about to perform Bach's Keyboard Concerto no. 1 in D Minor with the Queens College Orchestra, he called and left a ticket for her at the box office. She didn't attend, and he never heard from her again. Decades later, the memory of it still made him cry.

Rothman was a proponent of the Taubman Approach, a technique frequently embraced by pianists who have been injured. The Taubman method is an ergonomic way of playing that relies on changing body alignment and balance, using the laws of physiology to rewrite physical movement—a sort of yoga for piano. Advocates say it opens the door to an effortless technique. They hail it as a way to overcome technical limit-ations, as well as a cure for fatigue and playing-related injur-ies. Rothman had studied the Taubman method years before and incorporated one of its core components, circular wrist movement (a gentle rolling of the wrists), into his playing. He encouraged me to incorporate it, as it would help get rid of the tension that he identified in my arms and wrists. Whenever I became nervous, I tensed my arms, my muscles drew tight, and my playing turned brittle. The tension was subverting my music making. Rothman explained it like this: When a cat is at rest, it can pounce at any minute. A pianist's muscles needed to be similarly at the ready. I was to use the wrist as a fulcrum, making a small circular motion of the hand as I played through a passage. He scribbled "CW," short for circu-lar wrist, throughout the scores of music I was playing. But try as I might, I wasn't able to assimilate the technique. Maybe it was because we tried to change it in isolation, in small doses during the lesson, while continuing to work on Bach or Brahms. I would later learn that when pianists undertake the Taubman method, they typically stop playing altogether, sometimes for as long as a year, while they work on deconstructing and rebuilding their technique. Rothman wasn't suggesting I do that, but my inability to incorporate his teaching was becoming a frustration to both of us.

More important, Rothman had seen me trip up at several low-key student recitals, and I suspected that he had marked me as a poor performer, perhaps an incurably poor one. At one of his recitals, he welcomed the students and their guests, then asked who among us suffered the pangs of stage fright. All but the very youngest raised their hands. For the next several minutes, he ruminated on the causes and symptoms of performance anxiety—the rebellion of the fingers, he called it—and why it was so critical to face our terror. I wondered if I were being set up. By the time he finished talking, I was in a sweat. When my turn came, I played so badly—missing octave jumps, sliding into wrong notes, halting, forgetting, and crashing—that it sounded to my own ears as if I had never prepared. All those long hours of practice, wasted. As I stood and walked away from the piano, I saw Rothman bestow a look of pity on me. And suddenly I resented this beloved teacher. I was afraid he would always see me in that light, waiting for me to lose my way and stumble. That wasn't what I needed. I needed a teacher who saw my faults but recognized my potential, too.

In June 2012, around the time of the strange dreams, I began to search in a systematic way, auditioning for a handful of piano teachers within driving distance. Each audition was different: Some teachers sat beside me, almost touching, as they watched my hands and turned my pages; one sat far removed, like a member of an invisible audience. Yet another, a Russian pedagogue with a thick accent, directed me to a piano in a dark corner of his house. "You will play the Brahms," he declared when I had finished playing through my repertoire. "You will not play this Bach fugue; you will play a different one."

In the Vedic tradition, the philosophy behind classical yoga, a person without a guru is an orphan. I yearned for a teacher who would serve as my guru, who would take me seriously, push me to be the best I could be, and not give up on me because I was middle-aged, because my hands were small, because I couldn't do circular wrist. But all my effort at change had exposed me as a creature of habit. I had long prided myself on being an adventurous spirit, always ready to move to a new house, a new city, a new job. Wasn't I the person who once underlined Jacques Lacan, the French neo-Freudian psychoanalyst, when he warned against "the armor of an alienating identity"? If we move through our lives with too strong a sense of our own identity, he said, we exclude other possibilities.

But my possibilities at the piano seemed so limited. Whenever I tried to change my posture or even remind myself to keep breathing through a piece, I hit a wall. If I was being honest about it, I'd always been a slave to habit. Now, as I tried to draw back my shoulders and relax my wrists and fore-arms, I remembered sitting at my wooden desk in grade three, trying to learn how to hold a fountain pen. I had it wrapped under my thumb, covered with my pointer finger—making the kind of girl fist that will get your hand broken if you try to throw a punch. There was a hole for the inkwell in the upper right corner of the desk; we would not be permitted to graduate on to ballpoint until we had mastered the ability to write neatly with a fountain pen. And now the teacher was heading right for me. I was terrified of her, and for good reason. Miss Knisley regularly punished the boys for misdemeanors both great and small, like coming in late from recess. Once, as the class watched in silence, she lined up the culprits at the front of the class and flogged their hands with a supple inch-thick leather strap. But first, she made a great show of wetting down their hands, since, as she informed us with scientific detachment, pain and touch were more exquisite when the hands were lubricated. Other times, she locked girls and boys alike in the cloakroom, where she often forgot us, sometimes for the rest of the school day and once until evening, when Billy McBirnie's parents called the principal to inquire where their son had gotten. Now, as she patrolled the aisles, examining our hand position, Miss Knisley slapped my hand and pulled the fingers apart. I adjusted my pen hold that day, but by the next day I was holding it in the same clenched manner. I hold it the same way to this day.

If I couldn't change my penmanship, how reasonable was it to think I could change my body's response to terror? In practice sessions, I had been focusing on my wrists and arms, attempting to turn them into the relaxed muscles of a rag doll. I had tried going out for long runs, breathing through the music like a singer, loosening my mouth, jaw, and shoulders. None of it worked.

Having staked out the next year as my piano year, I began finding pianists everywhere I went. It was like when I bought my first Volvo station wagon in 1989; suddenly, every other car on the road was a Volvo. Now, everybody I met was a pianist. A couple of them had even arranged recitals to celebrate their fiftieth or sixtieth birthdays. Originality, alas, was not to be mine.

One of my new piano friends came recommended as a house sitter, willing to walk our dog in exchange for a decent piano to practice on. Lynn Kidder carried herself with an old-fashioned bearing. Unlike me, she rarely cursed; she exuded a ladylike reserve until she laughed, a big belly laugh that took no mind of what anybody else might think. She walked slowly, which was something I noticed but didn't think much about until she mentioned that she was recovering from an eleven-year bout of chronic fatigue syndrome triggered by mercury poisoning. It began after a dentist replaced a gold crown with one that contained a different mix of metals. The new mix leached mercury from older, nearby amalgam fillings into her bloodstream, and within a few weeks Kidder could barely sit upright. She forgot how to read (music and English), lived on yogurt, bananas, and bagels, required a caretaker to do her shopping and simple household chores, and struggled to make a long-distance phone call. She went from working as a computer programmer, building and designing a database, to the point where, as she put it, she couldn't add two plus three. It was four years before she got a diagnosis, at which point she had all her fillings removed and replaced with mercury-free compounds.

She spent a year getting chelation therapy to remove the heavy metal from her bloodstream, then languished for several more years with chronic fatigue syndrome before discovering neurolinguistic programming; amygdala retraining, she called it. When I met her, she was still recuperating and figured that she was about halfway back to her old self. I thought she was already extremely clever. A master knitter, she designed her own sweaters and knitted up intricate patterns for a boutique yarn shop, in exchange for fine and costly wool. She was an accomplished pianist who held a master's degree in performance from the University of Washington. As a young woman, she had dreamed of a concertizing career. But she lacked the necessary technique and eventually stopped playing in her thirties, choosing instead to move into a Seattle spiritual community that was affiliated with the sustainability movement.

Kidder, now in her fifties, was back in California and playing the piano again. Despite the fact that she lacked the energy to practice more than fifteen minutes at a time, she was determined to become a concert pianist and perform in every state west of the Rockies. I didn't tell her I thought this even more far-fetched than my own goal of performing a full-length public recital. Later, when I heard her play the piano, I reconsidered. She was an emotional person who could bring herself to tears as she recalled the tortured life of Chopin. She played with a plush tone that was full of unplugged joy and feeling. Kidder had told me that technique wasn't her strong suit, but I saw in an instant that it far surpassed my own.

We began getting together just to play for each other. I tried out a Brahms intermezzo, a piece that for me was still a work in progress. "You are a wonderful pianist," she told me. Her words took me by surprise; I was so startled by them, I began to cry. I felt like an impostor, I admitted. I was about to say more, but she stopped me, made me sit in a chair and touch the tip of my right thumb to the inner corner of my right eye. Now, she said, touch your fourth finger to the inner corner of your left eye, so that both fingertips are on either side of the bridge of your nose. Place the tip of your middle finger in between the two, above your eyebrows, and put your other hand on the back of your head, palm touching the head with thumb resting at the base of the skull. Repeating after her, I said, "I've had problems performing in the past, but I am a different person now."

Think about the worst thing that can happen, she continued. It wasn't hard to imagine: I pictured myself breaking down over the keyboard and running offstage before a hall full of judges. Let go of it, she ordered. Thank the universe for freeing you. Now, look at a point on the ceiling. Bow your head and frown, imagining your worst fears; look up at a fixed point in the ceiling, and yell, Stop! Stop! Stop! Then break out into a wide smile and cry: Yes! I did it!

I found these affirmations embarrassing, but I also began tearing up as I frowned into my lap. Kidder was a great believer in something she called "energy medicine," which gave her a lot of comfort and, she was convinced, real help through her years of sickness. She was especially attached to a therapy called "EFT" (Emotional Freedom Technique), which involved a lot of finger tapping, mostly on the head and face, while speaking aloud such phrases as "I deeply and completely accept myself." I didn't like the sensation of tapping on my head and face. It made me feel like a dead tree in which a woodpecker had taken up residence. Yet Kidder was such a competent, talented person and she seemed so sure of what she was offering, I was loath to dismiss her approach altogether. I trusted her when she insisted that all I needed was the right teacher. When the right one came along, she said, I would feel as if I were being adopted by a new parent.

As it happened, I was scheduled to audition for a teacher whom I had heard about through the music grapevine. Ellen Tryba Chen lived forty minutes away in Saratoga, across the mountain that locals call "the hill." A former artistic director of the Bay Area's Steinway Society, she knew all the best piano teachers in Silicon Valley. If she didn't think she was the right teacher for me, she'd know who was. But first she needed to hear me play. It was a Sunday afternoon in late June when I pulled up to her house, and the sound of the piano—she was working on the Grieg sonata—filtered through windows sealed against the early summer heat. When she opened the door, she was impeccably dressed. I later recognized that she always appeared like this: hair coiffed, trousers creased, with a well-tailored, color-coordinated blouse. It was a style acquired during a long residence in Tokyo, where she took careful note of some of the best-dressed women in the world. She was determined that her students see her as a professional. Her husband, Otis, was an engineer-turned-businessman who had moved from the aerospace industry to semiconductors and was now involved in renewable energy. He had just flown in over the weekend and lay crashed out in front of the TV at the other end of the house. I'd already heard they had a bicontinental marriage; he worked in Shanghai, where they had a condo and she visited several times a year. Occasionally, they met up in Germany, where one of their sons lived.

Ellen spilled over with ideas, often getting so excited by her thoughts that she would run off on a tangent. Stage fright! She knew all about stage fright. Did she mention that she used to break out in an allergic reaction after every performance in graduate school? An antihistamine breakdown: uncontrolled sneezing, running eyes, leaky nose. Did I have a technique for memorizing music? She would teach me her fail-safe method,

Ellen Chen (Courtesy of Kenneth Quan)

but not this time, another time. Ellen thought cosmically, saw connections, and seemed to read as much as I did. She typically taught until ten at night, after which she liked to relax over a Victorian novel by Anthony Trollope or Mrs. Gaskell. She asked me what I hoped to play at my concert, and when I mentioned the *Bagatelles* by Alexander Tcherepnin, she laughed with delight and told me she had played for Tcherepnin at a music festival in Wisconsin when she was seven years old. She loved his *Bagatelles*.

Here was the Sancho Panza to my Don Quixote. I wasn't just tilting at windmills, she assured me. She didn't see any reason I shouldn't succeed, she said, after hearing me play: Bach, then Brahms and Debussy. I was musical, I had a solid musical background, I had the tools. She wanted to go on this journey with me, and she was already brainstorming how to do it. I needed to practice performing in front of people, and one of the places I could do that was at the Mineta San Jose International Airport, where a baby grand sat just outside the edge of the Southwest Airlines baggage carousels. She was taking her young students to play there in a few weeks. Did I want to join them? And while she was thinking of it, there was also a concert grand in the ballroom at Filoli, a Georgian country estate with public gardens in nearby Woodside. She intended to find out if I could play it for visitors. Of course, she'd accompany me; we could take turns playing.

Sitting on the bench of one of her two side-by-side Mason & Hamlin seven-footers, I decided she was the most intense and demanding teacher I'd ever met. I was glad that I'd remembered to take a beta-blocker to quell my nerves. Now, as I played some more, she perched herself across the room on a desk, following the music in her own score, sipping tea brewed in a Japanese pot. I would discover that was how she routinely conducted her lessons. Not bad, she'd say, articulating the words with a slurred, almost singsong phrase. It was one of her great compliments. In the months to come, it could send me into paroxysms of joy that I tried to contain, largely because I knew she would always have something more to add. I could practice a piece until I thought it was perfect, bring it to her, and realize with a hard letdown that we were just at the beginning of exploring its secrets. I had barely begun to understand it. Learning the notes and getting it up to speed, playing with the proper dynamics and feeling, figuring out the articulation—that was just the beginning. I had never gone this deeply into music, or anything for that matter, before meeting Ellen Tryba Chen. Other teachers had heard me play a Bach fugue or Brahms intermezzo and concluded that I was ready to move on to the next piece. Not Ellen. At first I felt dismayed, as if I had failed. Then I felt irked, and I told myself that I was being nitpicked to death. At the end of one intense session, a lesson lasting nearly two hours, I mentioned that I had spent a lot of time working on that Bach fugue; I hadn't expected her to find so much wrong with it. She looked at me, her mouth open in surprise, for once slow to respond with words. In that moment, I knew that I had found exactly what I had gone searching for: a teacher who was willing to work with me as a serious student. Every musical phrase was up for analysis; no note was too minor to take for granted.

My biggest challenge, she informed me, was my tension. Rothman, of course, had told me the same. She said I had a fierce dedication to getting the notes right; it was getting in the way of my touch. Another time she chastised me for seeking her approval. Don't look at me for approval, she scolded. Look to yourself. I felt like a child.

Mostly, I appreciated her for the intensity of her feelings. Once, after she saw András Schiff perform Bach's *English Suites* from memory in San Francisco, she stood on her tiptoes in front of her piano, placed a hand on her heart, and said, "I felt the way you do with your own child, that if any harm came to him, I would lay down my life." I understood that kind of passion, that reach for hyperbole when nothing else would do. It spoke to a depth of feeling that could also over-whelm me after a great, transformative performance.

Ellen soon became my biggest inspiration. After a couple of weeks of lessons, we met up at the airport in San Jose, where I found her in Terminal B, surrounded by schoolchildren, her students. Their parents sat in nearby plastic chairs, drinking coffee, reading books and newspapers. As travelers strode past, pulling suitcases and talking on cell phones, Ellen opened "the recital," playing a Spanish dance by Enrique Granados. She was an exciting pianist to watch, not just technically excellent but full of verve. The piano had a tinny sound that was muffled by a barrage of public announcements, but she took no mind. The kids played next, and then it was my turn.

This had happened way too fast. I wasn't ready. I forced myself to sit at the piano and play a Debussy prelude. Ellen later told me that I looked and sounded like a robot. As soon as I finished, I began gathering up my things to say good-bye. "Where are you going?" she demanded. "You've just begun." We kept at it all afternoon, as Ellen cycled us through our pieces. The children played, their parents clapped, and then it was my turn again. It got kind of boring. It was no big deal. I grew relaxed. Then, just when I thought that I could finally go home, Ellen announced that we were moving on to Terminal A, where a little upright piano stood in an alcove next to security. This piano was even worse than the other, but as we rotated through our pieces I realized that I was feeling as much at ease in this ugly corner of the airport as in my living room. I would have done anything for Ellen Chen at that moment. I began to thank her, but I couldn't talk because I realized I was crying. So was she.

Chapter 5

MASSAGING THE OCTOPUS

"THE BULLETPROOF MUSICIAN" was one of the first items to pop up on my screen when I typed in the words *music performance anxiety*. It was the website of Noa Kageyama, a New York psychologist and violinist who works with musicians from around the world, coaching them for auditions, concerts, and competitions and training them in focus techniques and ways to cope with performance anxiety. Stage fright could not only be managed, he asserted; it could be turned into an asset: "The specific mental skills you develop will allow you to experience the satisfaction of performing up to your abilities—even when the lights are brightest ... *Especially when the lights are brightest.*" The key was in learning to reprogram one's response to stress, and he offered a *bullet-proof* approach based on years of performance psychology research plus his own experience and training. When I learned that the Juilliard School, his alma mater, had hired him to teach this approach, I lost no time contacting him. He agreed to work with me almost at once, and by June 2012 we had begun meeting weekly via Skype—he from the hallway of his

Upper West Side apartment in Manhattan, I from my home office in California.

Kageyama told me he had been given his first violin, a Cracker Jack box fitted with a ruler for a fingerboard, when he was two years old. Though it was he who requested it, the instrument quickly became the focus of his mother's ambitions. She read everything that Shinichi Suzuki, founder of the world-famous Suzuki method, had to say about teaching music to children. She was especially taken by one of his axioms—that practicing music was like eating. A person does not eat one big meal a week, Suzuki wrote. He needs to nourish himself every day. So, too, with practicing. The mother interpreted this to mean that if her son didn't practice, he didn't eat. There was at least one time the boy didn't eat.

When Noa was five, she pulled him out of kindergarten in rural Ohio so they could fly to Matsumoto, Japan, to study directly with the master. After months of letters, telegrams, and international phone calls, Suzuki had agreed to accept him as a student. Kageyama remembers a large studio hazy with cigarette smoke and a kindly man in a pressed suit conducting an orchestra of three or four hundred child violinists, all sawing away at the same piece, *La Folia* by Arcangelo Corelli. During one performance, Suzuki became so animated that he stepped back and fell off the stage. "I forgot to wind myself up today," Kageyama recalls the old man joking as he popped back up and performed a jig, like a wind-up doll, for the surprised children.

Mostly, Kageyama recalls the stress of working on the same challenging piece of music, day after day, during the six months he lived in Japan. It wasn't just the music. "It was very stressful being away from my culture, my language, and my father," he says now. "My mother had invested so much time and money and effort to make it happen. It became very serious very quickly. When I came home, I knew this was work, a very serious thing. There were practice logs every single day, but instead of checklists my mom tried to make it fun with smiley faces." The little boy wasn't fooled, and there were many afternoons that he ran away, escaping into the cornfields behind his house. When he returned, the violin was always waiting.

Today, Kageyama can appreciate that his mother's ambitions were more about her than him; as her only child, he just happened to be in the crosshairs. She was an *Issei*, a first-generation Japanese immigrant, who had been eclipsed in childhood by her sister. The older girl had been the beneficiary of all the family's resources, the one who received art lessons and a top-notch education and who went on to become a visual artist of some repute in Japan. By the time his mother came along, the family's resources had dried up. "I wonder," he said to me, "if it was like that for your mom as well."

The question took me by surprise.

While his mother's outsize drive was out of proportion to anything I knew, there was something more than vaguely familiar about it. My mother was the third daughter of Russian Jewish immigrants. Her oldest sister, Madeline, studied piano at Eastman while her other sister, Bessie, attended the University of Buffalo and dreamed of making it big in advertising. By the time my mother graduated from high school, the family had gone broke in the Depression and she had to go to work to help support her parents.

When, as a child, I refused to practice, she used to chase me around the dining room table with a long-handled wooden spoon. She was fast on her feet, and she caught me so many times that it became a running joke. I don't remember it hurting much, but I do remember that she broke a lot of spoons on me. Whenever she did, she'd call my father to matter-of-factly request that he pick up a new one on his way home. As other women might ask their husbands to stop off for a gallon of milk.

Kageyama's mother took her zeal to another level. While he was still in elementary school, she had him read Anthony Robbins's book *Awakening the Giant Within: How to Take Immediate Control of Your Mental, Emotion, Physical and Financial Destiny*. Every other week, she drove eight hours to Chicago in order for him to study with Roland and Almita Vamos, two of the top violin and viola teachers in the world. When he was fourteen, she accompanied him to the Aspen Music Festival, which he attended on a fellowship for the next nine summers.

He was unusually, preternaturally, gifted, but it was a gift he did not want. By the time he arrived at the Oberlin Conservatory in 1994, his first order of business was to cut loose from the school orchestra. Free of his mother's over-sight, he spent his days hanging out with friends, playing video games, and making his way to the practice room for maybe an hour or two in the evenings. In a world of striving young musicians, for whom five-hour practice logs are a daily baseline, his take-it-or-leave-it attitude unnerved his fellow students. When in his senior year he won the school's concerto competition, none of the judges knew who he was; in four years, he had never played in the orchestra.

Still, it never occurred to him that he didn't have to play the violin. His life had been laid down on a set of tracks that ran in only one direction, and he couldn't imagine getting off. Without really thinking about it, in 1998 he headed to Juilliard in New York. It would prove a miserable experience. "Most people come around and realize they care about music, love the violin, and thank their parents," he said. "That never happened to me." His epiphany came during a dinner with classmates, when the conversation turned to what they'd do if they ever won the lottery. One said she'd start a musical festival. Someone else mentioned a music foundation. Kagayema didn't have to think twice about his answer: He would put down his violin and never touch it again.

Then, in his second semester, he took a class with Don Greene, a former Green Beret who served as sport psychologist for the U.S. Olympic Diving Team and the World Championship swimming team. Greene had been invited by a voice teacher at Juilliard to help prepare four students for their auditions with the Metropolitan Opera Orchestra. Of the fifty-nine candidates who sang at the audition, his four protégés came in first, second, fourth, and fifth. The results were so impressive that Juilliard talked Greene into joining its faculty. His presence would have huge repercussions for Kageyama, who, for all his success, recognized that he'd always played better in the practice room than in the performance hall. But he had no idea that there was a whole field dedicated to figuring out why that might be. He had studied psychology as an undergraduate—mostly, he says with a sly smile, to get out of orchestra—and what he'd learned was what mainstream psychology then promulgated about performance anxiety: that it was a social phobia. The term first made its appearance in the 1980 edition of the *Diagnostic and Statistical Manual of Mental Disorders*, where it was defined as intense anxiety during a performance, be it music, acting, dancing, public speaking, or anything else. The definition cast a wide net. It applied to shy people who froze at parties, as well as those who became paralyzed with fear when they ran into an acquaintance at Safeway. For a truly phobic person, even that sort of mundane event can feel like a major performance.

The definition has changed considerably over time, with the 2013 edition of the *DSM*, the fifth edition, cautioning that "performance anxiety, stage fright and shyness in social situations that involve unfamiliar people (a potentially hostile audience) are common and should not be diagnosed as social phobia unless the anxiety or avoidance leads to clinically significant impairment or marked distress." But while psychiatrists have argued over whether stage fright is a pathology, sport psychologists have long regarded it as a normal response to a high-stakes situation. They're not interested in eliminating anxiety; rather, they see it as a positive force, to be harnessed and roped into service, like Prometheus's gift of fire. Without it, Kageyama told me, there is no excitement, no passion, no peak performance. "Fear builds excitement. That sudden adrenaline burst? It's a signal of something important

Noa Kageyama (Courtesy of Ahlin Min)

that's about to happen. You're always going to be nervous. You just need to learn how to channel it."

Like his mentor Don Greene, Kageyama considers himself a sport psychologist—though one who works specifically with musicians, athletes of the small motor muscles. In that capacity, he initiated our sessions by having me complete an Inventory of Performance Skills, a questionnaire of eighty-four statements designed to gauge a musician's anxiety level. My answers underlined what I already knew about myself: "Going into performances, I expect to do well." (Not true.) "I feel bold onstage." (Hardly.) "I talk to myself in a positive way." (Not very true.) "I wish I could manage my nerves better." (Duh.) Overall, my scores showed me to be fearful and anxious, running away from whatever I found difficult or scary. Fear of failure left me tentative, hesitant, and inclined to play it safe, shying away from bold musical gestures and expressiveness. Not surprisingly, I scored low on resilience, revealing myself as someone who became so distracted by a slipup that I had trouble continuing with the music.

It was, Kageyama acknowledged months later, "one of the more extreme profiles" he had seen. How bad was it? I prodded. He smiled, looking as if he were about to crack a joke on late-night TV, then caught himself and offered up the word *challenging*. I did my best, he told me, when I wasn't completely calm. I thrived on some excitement, some adrenaline. I wasn't happy at ninety miles an hour, but it was also clear that I didn't function at thirty. I was a just-under-the-speed-limit pianist—forty-five miles an hour. There were a lot of problems in my profile: I lacked confidence, I avoided opportunities, I had difficulty focusing my mind on the music. On the other hand, I was capable of summoning my resources in a pinch and showed great determination.

Act and think like the person you want to be, he urged. Record your playing every day and then listen to it intently without critiquing or analyzing the music. Learn to really listen. Sing along while playing, as Glenn Gould used to do. (If you listen carefully—and sometimes not so carefully—you can hear him, humming along on his recordings in a low, near constant drone.) Kageyama called it "singing brain."

These were the tools of cognitive behavior therapy, a psychodynamic approach aimed at driving home emotional insights with clear goal-oriented targets. Kageyama wasn't interested in why I had stage fright; as far as he was concerned, everybody had it. The key, he said, was learning how to "center," how to better cultivate a sense of interior calm. When I figured out how to do that, the anxiety of performing would melt away. He himself learned how to do it when he was a student at Juilliard, preparing for an international competition. As usual, he hadn't prepared nearly enough. He was nervously pacing his apartment when he came upon a brochure about the powers of centering. As he studied it, he recalled the visualization exercises and other mental games his mother had instilled, and he quickly figured out what he needed to do. When he played at the competition, the result surprised him. "I wasn't even prepared, but given my level of preparation I hit it out of the park—way beyond where I had any right to." He made it to the second round, then realized that if he made it any further, he would have to disqualify himself. He hadn't bothered to learn the required repertoire.

By this point, though, it didn't matter. He had just been introduced to "the zone," and it was all he cared about. "Once you get there and you realize what it feels like, you don't ever want to perform anywhere else than that," he said. "Because it's just too nerve-racking to do so. Once you figure out where your ideal zone is, what you're paying attention to, that's the only thing that ends up mattering. When there were times I couldn't get there for some reason, how I played actually mattered less to me than getting to that place where I knew I could play well."

Kageyama had ideas about how to help me find my own zone, but first he wanted me to write up an identity statement, a short mantra that would couple my greatest strength with my aspirations. It would be a way of linking something that was already true with something I hoped to make true. When, at our next session, I read my statement aloud ("My energy is formidable and I am the most magnetic amateur pianist in the Bay Area"), I could barely deliver it with a straight face. I was instructed to print it out, tape it to the bathroom mirror, and repeat it aloud every time I looked in the mirror. It will be your mantra, he told me, a personal affirmation that will drive you forward. The thought of seeing such silliness posted on my bathroom mirror made me cringe.

"We have this idea of who we think we are, and it's not correct," Kageyama went on, and assigned me to draw up a list of my top ten courageous moments. "If you look at that list, you'll see what you're capable of."

I fretted over this second assignment, trying to come up with items that were worthy of inclusion. I considered the act of natural childbirth, which I'd managed to pull off three times, but crossed it off when I realized that both my grandmothers had accomplished the same and neither would have called herself courageous for doing so. Other occasions came to mind: moving to Italy to work as an au pair when I could barely speak Italian, hitchhiking across the United Kingdom, hauling lobsters in Scotland. But including them struck me as cheating: In my late teens and early twenties, these escapades had been taken as larks. Everyone I'd met on my summer swings through Europe had been kind and solicitous—one old Scotswoman going so far as to invite me into her house, where she drew up a hot bath and set out an enormous breakfast of fried kippers and haggis. These were stories I told to give my life a certain flair.

But there was one story I didn't tell, mostly because forty years after the fact, I still felt ashamed of my part in it. It happened when I was sixteen, hitchhiking from the summer camp in northern Ontario where I was a counselor to Toronto. The man who picked me up appeared pleasant and nonthreatening. He told me he had been driving all night from Sault Ste. Marie, a city far to the north. He was willing to take me all the way into Toronto, but first he wanted to stop off at his house in the suburbs, say hello to his wife and kids, and change his shirt. When I heard that he had a wife, I imagined I was safe and agreed. Of course, there was no one in the house. He made me a sandwich (roast beef with ketchup on Wonder Bread) and made a phone call to someone named Paul. Then, as I was finishing up my sandwich, he locked the kitchen door and dragged me through the hall, past the photographs of his children in their school uniforms, and into his bedroom. I opened my mouth to scream and nothing came out. My vocal cords were frozen. I was frozen. He threw me on the bed and I managed to whisper, "I have a boyfriend." It was a ridiculous thing to say; in fact, I didn't have a boyfriend, I'd never had a boyfriend, and even if I had, why would it make any difference? He took off his shirt and rolled on top of me. I caught a glimpse of a framed photograph of his wife in her wedding dress, and I squeaked out the only question that made sense in the moment: How can you do this to your wife? I'm not doing it to her, he said, I'm doing it to you. He said it almost grimly, but with humor—as if he were getting to a chore that he'd put off much too long but that really wasn't so bad. His words hit me like a bucket of ice water. I instantly came to life and did the only thing left to me: I sank my teeth deep into his arm, as far as they could sink. Sometimes even now, when I close my eyes, I can remember the taste of that flaccid, pink flesh and recall the way he howled and fell away, leaving me to jump up and make my escape.

Yes, I thought, that was courageous. I would give myself that. I had walked away, moved on, and pushed myself out into the world—traveling, working, taking risks without excessive fear for my physical safety. Why, then, whenever I sat down at the piano to play for an audience, no matter how small, did I tremble like a cornered animal? My heart pounded as wildly as if I were being attacked—but the one time I *was* attacked, I'd risen to the occasion. The girl who could save herself from being raped, with no weapon other than her teeth, was surely capable of summoning up some reserve of courage at the piano.

The existential psychologist Rollo May defined anxiety as "a threat to some value that the individual holds essential to his existence as a personality." That definition is hard to apply to a fear of spiders, snakes, heights, or bridges, but it is central to a fear of performance. Asking myself which of my own essential values were threatened, I saw the answer: There sat my mother in the audience. I'd swallowed her values whole. For years, she had conveyed that music was the best part of me. If I failed at the piano, what did that signify?

Kageyama said I should do something every day that was outside my comfort zone. We would rate the activities on a scale of one to ten, beginning on a three and working my way up from there. We would structure them into an adventure. Ever since my first airport "recital" with Ellen Chen, I had begun dropping by Terminal B in San Jose. "My energy is formidable and I am the most magnetic amateur pianist in the Bay Area," I whispered to myself as I laid out my books of music: Bach, Brahms, Debussy, Tcherepnin, and Piazzolla. Kageyama deemed it a seven on the adventure scale.

After a few of these performances, I occasionally forgot about my mantra. Sometimes, a small audience of skycaps,

Sara playing piano at San Jose International Airport (Shmuel Thaler)

baggage handlers, and travelers with time to kill grew around me, and as they sipped their Peet's coffees, I played my heart out. Once, when I stood up and gathered my things, they actually applauded and called out their thanks. I thought of my mantra, which suddenly seemed all wrong. I went home and wrote up another: "I am someone who has begun to overcome her fears and I enjoy playing for people and bringing them beautiful music." It wasn't much better, but it didn't make me cringe.

After three months of weekly Skype sessions, Kageyama suggested it was time to dial up to number eight on the adventure scale. At his urging, I signed up for the Sonata Workshop, a piano camp in a sprawling Bennington, Vermont, manor house that had once been a nuns' convent and now held a piano in every room. Over eight days, I would cycle through almost every one of those pianos, practicing in linen closets, bedrooms, a laundry room, the basement, and the living room. The place was filled with piano-obsessed people, all pursuing their passion with unique single-mindedness, playing piano, listening to piano, and talking piano from the moment they woke up till the time they went to bed. "What kind of pianist are you?" one competitive guy demanded at breakfast early in the week. I must have looked perplexed because he clarified and threw out the names of other campers for comparison purposes: "On a scale of one to ten, where two is a beginner, five is a Carolyn, and nine is a Keith, where are you?" I stared at him, wondering if I had unwittingly set myself up for yet another music competition.

One of my roommates was a twenty-eight-year-old woman who had never before played the piano. Fatimah Muhammad grew up homeless in New Jersey. She lived on the streets and in shelters with her brother and mother, who was determined that her children get an education. In 2006, Muhammad graduated Phi Beta Kappa from the University of Pennsylvania. A few months before arriving at the Sonata Workshop, she had come within four hundred votes of unseating a twenty-seven-year incumbent in the Democratic primary for a seat in the Pennsylvania State Senate. She had a powerful gospel-tinged voice, and she had toured India, Malaysia, and China, singing jazz and blues before thousands. Her mother had recently died of breast cancer, and a couple of times that week I woke in the middle of the night to the sound of her sobs. She said she didn't know what exactly she wanted to do with her life, except that whatever it was, it would involve music. When she performed on the last night, it was to accompany herself in a song she had composed. She was nervous (she'd actually thrown up before going on), and she touched her hand to her heart "to check in" before belting out a glorious number. I watched as she arched a hand above the keys, the gesture of a confident pianist, and I decided that her vulnerability was actually a mask that concealed great strength.

A lot of people at the camp had powerful stories. One, Tony Cicoria, was already famous, having been profiled by the neurologist Oliver Sacks in the *New Yorker* as the man who at forty-two years of age developed an insatiable appetite for classical piano music after being struck by lightning. An orthopedic surgeon in a small city in upstate New York, he was talking on a pay phone in 1994 when a flash of electricity burst out of the receiver and hit him in the face. The next thing he knew, he was getting CPR from the woman who had been next in line. A bluish-white light bathed him, and he was hovering over his own body, overcome with a feeling of peace and well-being. Then, with a *whoosh*, he was back on the ground, covered with burns on his face and feet.

For the next few weeks, he was sluggish and forgetful. Medical tests found nothing amiss, however, and he resumed his life as a doctor and family man until one morning he woke up and felt an inexplicable desire to hear classical music. Before the lightning strike, he had had no such interest; if he listened to anything, it was rock. He began to buy recordings of classical pianists—Vladimir Ashkenazy was his favorite— and listened obsessively. When his son's babysitter moved away, she stored her piano, "a nice little upright," in Cicoria's house. Cicoria began to take lessons and play whenever he had a few minutes to spare. Music was a constant presence in his head, like an audio file, which he could stop and start on command. When I met him, he seemed a man obsessed, attacking the keys with alarming ferocity whether he was playing Beethoven's *Moonlight* Sonata or the piano concerto he had recently composed. It was called *The Lightning Concerto* and it was very intense.

Another of my roommates was a California nursing professor who on first impression seemed brash and outgoing. As I soon discovered, she was as terrified of performing as I was. Irene Larsen promised she would sign up for a master class if I did. "Why not?" she said with a toss of her head. "It's the things you don't buy, the things you don't say, the people you don't tell to fuck off—those are the regrets in life." She never did sign up for the master class. But without allowing myself to think about it, I added my name to the list.

This meant that I would have to play before all twenty-six pianists in attendance, after which my playing would be dissected, in public, by Polly van der Linde, the camp director. She was pure energy. An excellent pianist, she could sight-read almost anything that was put in front of her. She could also read people. She had an uncanny way of zeroing in on the strengths and weaknesses of their playing, without ever talking down or seeming to compromise her own standards.

The afternoon of my master class, I took a long walk on a country road, past picturesque farmhouses and rolling hills. Drivers tore past me, one nearly brushing me. I saw myself struck dead, a piece of roadkill as cars whizzed past my lifeless body. At least I wouldn't have to play in the master class, I considered, a thought that brought to mind a story about Pablo Casals. When the cellist visited San Francisco in 1901, he suffered a serious injury to his bowing hand during a hike up Mount Tamalpais, the highest point in Marin County, just across the Golden Gate Bridge. A large rock had fallen on his hand, crushing several fingers. The first thought that came to his mind, Casals later said, was, "Thank God, I'll never have to play the cello again!"

I returned to the house unharmed, without any excuse to keep me from playing the Brahms rhapsody that evening. That was a pity. After six bars, I broke down and went back to the beginning. Remembering Kageyama, I took a slow breath and started over, trying to focus on the good things: my tone, my passion—my formidable energy. I played accurately for another page or two, and then—*kaboom*—I flubbed the ending. When it was over, I sat on the bench trying not to cry, awaiting van der Linde's decree. It didn't take her long. "You can handle the piano," she said. "You just can't handle yourself at the piano." My fellow students laughed, some a little nervously, but at that moment I felt like throwing my arms around her. I was thrilled to be called out as an emotional mess; I just couldn't stand being dismissed as a pianist.

Later, she told me about one of her longtime students, an older man named George who many years earlier had given up all hope of a music career. He attended the Oberlin Conservatory but quit performing because of his stage fright and instead spent his life as a corporate executive. The piano bug never left him, however, and every year he came to the Sonata Workshop, where, predictably, he was overcome by nerves. Once, van der Linde coaxed him onstage with a bit of humor; she placed a huge sombrero on his head. It helped. Another time, she shared with him her own past experiences in a chamber group: how, before a performance, she and the other players, all scared stiff, huddled backstage like players on a football team. "We're great, yeah, yeah, yeah! Merry Christmas and fuck you!"

George listened attentively. The next evening, he walked onstage, bowed to his audience, and let loose a scroll—like a court jester in a Monty Python movie—that announced in big block letters: FUCK YOU! He played brilliantly.

I decided to go for broke at the final recital and wrote down a series of commandments that I studied like a tip sheet for a test.

Breathe. Don't stop!
Don't hunch shoulders
Loosen mouth
Focus—If drift, STOP!
Play from the heart

Listening to my fellow pianists that night, I was aware of the rise and fall of the breath beneath their back muscles and shoulders, the tapping of their feet, their bopping heads, the clunky playing of one, the gentle music of another, the boldness and confidence of a few. It was like finding oneself in the middle of a nudist colony, surrounded by the diversity of human bodies: the poking ribs, the rolls of fat, the solid thighs. I loved these people! And as I began my own piece, Debussy's *Reflets dans l'eau (Reflections in the Water)*, I knew exactly what I wanted to do with it. It was a demanding piece that had to sound ephemeral, like flowing water, a river of music: gushing, rippling, eddying. I'd been playing it for about two months, not long enough for my fingers to be entirely comfortable with Debussy's cascading runs. Yet as I played that night in Vermont, I had a vision of the way *Reflets* could sound—and there were times when my playing felt alive, matching the vision. There were even passages that seemed easy: I had found my zone, however briefly. Afterward, people told me I had played beautifully, that I had created magic for long minutes. I didn't know the name of the piece, one woman said, but it sounded like water. Another woman urged me to enter the Seattle International Piano Festival & Competition, of which she was an organizer. "I don't know what your standards of success are, Sara," van der Linde told me, "but in my book you succeeded. You played right from the heart."

Naturally, I was thrilled. But a couple of weeks later, I listened to a recording of myself from that evening and was disturbed. I could hear the tension in my body, the held breath, the panic that communicated its way from my lungs, through my arm muscles, down to my fingers, and into the key bed. At that moment, as I heard that playback, my goal changed. It no longer was about perfection. I could live with a missed note, a botched leap, a second's hesitation. What I couldn't live with was that tight little sound that crept into my playing. Fear makes one pull back and close in on oneself. It's a universal that the Tibetan Buddhist teacher Pema Chödrön identifies even in sea anemones, whose soft bodies close in on themselves the instant we touch them with our fingers. "It's not a terrible thing that we feel fear when faced with the unknown," she writes. "It is part of being alive, something we all share. We react against the possibility of loneliness, of death, of not having anything to hold on to. Fear is a natural reaction to moving closer to the truth."

The next time I Skyped with Kageyama, I told him about my experiences in Vermont—a ten on the adventure scale. I also confided my unexpected disappointment. He nodded. "It's more about self-discovery and mastery than anything else," he said. He was reminded of *Jiro Dreams of Sushi*, a documentary about an eighty-five-year-old sushi chef whose ten-seat, $300-a-plate restaurant was legendary among foodies the world over. While all the other sushi chefs in Tokyo massaged their octopi for a mere ten minutes, Jiro insisted that his be massaged for forty minutes—or he wouldn't serve them. "It's about how you have to love to massage the octopus before you serve it," Kageyama concluded.

I looked at the calendar. It was already September. Another eight months before my final recital. Suddenly, it no longer seemed like a lot of time. But at that moment, I felt that change was afoot: I was massaging the octopus.

Chapter 6

REVENGE OF THE AMYGDALA

FEAR: IT BEGINS WITH urgent motor impulses from the brain to the adrenal glands, which respond by dumping adrenaline into the bloodstream and putting the body on alert. The heart beats harder and faster. Breathing grows rapid to increase oxygen levels. Eyes dilate to bring more light to the retina, heightening visual acuity. Blood flow is redirected from hands and feet to the large muscles in the upper torso, arms, and legs. Hands and fingers turn cold and clammy. Sweat glands shift into overdrive. Digestion shuts down, and waves of nausea ripple through the gut. Hair follicles tighten, prompting individual hairs to bristle—an effect that likely made our hirsute Neanderthal ancestors appear larger and more menacing to predators.

It was the philosopher and psychologist William James who, in the 1880s, posed the first serious questions about the origins of fear: Do we run because we are afraid? Or are we afraid because we run? Which comes first? Does a person have time to contemplate whether something is frightening, or does the response to fear precede the thought? James had more than a passing interest in this chicken-or-egg conundrum. He was an anxiety-ridden insomniac (he regularly used chloroform to put himself to sleep)[1] and social phobic who, like many psychologists then and now, pursued a line of research that is sometimes only half-jokingly referred to as "me search." His conclusion was that emotion stems from the unconscious mind's perception of bodily changes—the adrenaline rush, the pounding heartbeat, the rapid breathing. In other words, action precedes consciousness. We are afraid because we run. To illustrate, he asked his readers to imagine an encounter with a bear: When we see a bear, we don't fear it and then run. We see it, run, and fear it—in that order.[2]

It would take more than a century for this insight to be confirmed in the laboratory, where Joseph LeDoux, a neuroscientist at New York University, mapped the circuitry of fear in lab rats, tracing it to the amygdala, an almond-shaped organ buried deep in the temporal lobe of the brain. LeDoux didn't go looking for the amygdala; he was looking for whatever region in the rat's auditory system was required for fear conditioning. He began his search by pairing a tone with an electric shock—a paradigm that has shaped the course of science experiments ever since Ivan Pavlov trained dogs to salivate at the sound of a bell. Once the rats were conditioned to associate the two, LeDoux dropped the shock and just sounded the tone. Again, classic: The rats froze in place the instant they heard the sound. It was their learned response to a tone that signaled danger.

Now LeDoux began cutting into the rodents' auditory cortex—the part of the auditory pathway associated with higher, rational thinking. The animals still froze whenever he sounded the tone; they were now terrified of a nonexistent electric shock and a noise they no longer consciously heard. LeDoux recognized that the auditory information must have split in the thalamus, a region in the lower brain that acts as a switching center for virtually all sensory information. But then what? Clearly, it traveled to some other part of the rat's brain, a part of the subconscious that could still process the tone. To find where, he injected a tracer chemical into the thalamus and waited for it to piggyback on molecules traveling onward to the mysterious terminus. When he dissected the rat's brain the next day, he laid it out under a microscope and found a stain of bright orange particles with streams and speckles against a dark blue-gray background. It was, he wrote, "like looking into a strange world of inner space. It was incredibly beautiful and I stayed glued to the microscope for hours."[3]

The stain had traveled to four regions of the brain. He resumed his cutting into the rats' brains, sounding the tone, cutting, and sounding the tone once again, until, by the process of elimination, he hit pay dirt: the amygdala. "We do not tremble because we are afraid or cry because we feel sad," LeDoux wrote, echoing William James. "We are afraid because we tremble and sad because we cry."

Without an amygdala, a rat loses all fear. In some experiments, amygdala-less rats (ones whose amygdalae have been surgically removed) happily clamber on top of sleeping cats and nip at their ears. A person whose amygdala is damaged can't recognize the expression of fear on another person's face.

The amygdala leaps into overdrive whenever we feel threatened. It is our internal guard dog, always on the lookout for a moving shadow, a slammed gate, a knock at the door. When an engine backfires on the street, the amygdala receives the information and makes us jump, ready to fight or flee, before the prefrontal cortex (the conscious brain) weighs in. The whole process takes twelve milliseconds, during which the amygdala waits around—like a brilliant math student marking time while her more ordinary classmates catch up—for the higher brain to run its processing and figure out if there's a problem.

Fear conditioning is not only lightning fast; it is the most effective learning. There is little forgetting when it comes to fear. That has been understood and even exploited for hundreds of years, as psychologist James McGaugh details in his 2003 book, *Memory and Emotion*:

"In medieval times, before writing was used to keep historical records, other means had to be found to maintain records of important events, such as the granting of land to a township, an important wedding or negotiations between powerful families. To accomplish this, a young child about seven years old was selected, instructed to observe the proceedings carefully, and then thrown into a river. In this way, it was said, the memory of the event would be impressed on the child and the record of the event maintained for the child's lifetime."[4]

One of the breakthroughs in understanding the link between fear and memory came in 1911, when Swiss neurologist and psychologist Édouard Claparède came across an amnesiac patient in a Geneva clinic. The woman retained all her old memories but was unable to create new ones. Though Claparède greeted her each day, she never remembered him; each time he entered her room, it was like a first meeting in which he had to introduce himself all over again. One day, he hid a pin in his hand and reached out to shake her hand, pricking her. The next day, as usual, she did not remember him. But when he went to shake her hand, she withheld it, recognizing a threat.[5]

That's because fear learning is laid down in the amygdala, separately from the learning of people's names, the Pythagorean theorem, or how to drive a stick shift. Most long-term memories reside in the hippocampus, where they have a tendency to weaken and dissolve over time. That little seahorse in the brain is one of the first regions affected by Alzheimer's disease. But fear memories can't afford to weaken, turn fallible, or go up in smoke. Our survival as a species depends on our ability to remember that the touch of a flame destroys, the bite of a rattlesnake is shot through with poison, and a charging hyena has murder on the brain. Sometimes there are no second chances. Evolution has done all it can to ensure that fear memories remain unshakable—"implicit" in neuroscience lingo, "unconscious" in Freudian. The amygdala is what keeps them that way. The stronger the emotional response signaled by the amygdala, the better the chance we'll remember it. With a single bad experience, we can become conditioned to fear things that are totally harmless. And it doesn't matter whether the threat is external or internal, real or imagined: The brain responds the same.

That fact begs a critical question: If fear learning is so powerful, how realistic is it to hope to overcome a lifetime of stage fright? Can the hapless musician or nerve-ridden actor retrain his or her amygdala and so reclaim some degree of poise? Or is it a fool's errand, destined to fail because of the very nature of fear acquisition? Scientists are addressing the broader question of whether fear can be reversed. Much of the research is funded by the U.S. Department of Defense, which has an obvious interest in the extinction of traumatic memories. Nearly three hundred thousand veterans from the wars in Iraq and Afghanistan have been diagnosed with post-traumatic stress disorder. Health care for a veteran with PTSD costs three and a half times as much as it does for one without the disorder. The human and financial toll is overwhelming, with medical care costs exceeding $2 billion. But the government's research holds potential far beyond the military. Anxiety disorders represent the most common mental illness in the country. They affect 18 percent of the adult population, or forty million people, according to the National Institute of Mental Health. In addition to PTSD, they include obsessive-compulsive disorder, panic disorder, generalized anxiety disorder, and social phobia (of which performance anxiety is a subset).

The most common form of treatment is known as "extinction training." In the laboratory, the idea is simple enough: Stop shocking the poor rat whenever it hears the tone and then repeat that pattern again and again and again—as many times as it takes for the animal to learn that the tone doesn't necessarily signal pain. Had LeDoux repeated his routine enough times, his rats might have behaved differently. Psychologists use the same approach with their clients, only they call it "exposure therapy." What they have learned, along with lab scientists, is that human anxieties and phobias are more resistant to extinction than animal fears. It's easier to get a rat to stop jumping at a buzzer than it is to get a phobic driver across the George Washington Bridge.

But exposure therapy remains the best treatment for anxiety disorders such as mine, according to Michael Fanselow, a neuroscientist at the University of California at Los Angeles. "When we're afraid, part of the fear response is an increase in blood pressure and heart rate. What often happens—and this is especially the case in public-performing fears—you get these changes, which in turn make the fear worse, which makes your blood pressure and heart rate go up even more. So you get into this positive feedback loop." He recommended a combination of beta-blockers and exposure training, which— coming as it did from one of the top neuroscientists in the country—hardly sounded like state-of-the-art advice.

Beta-blockers are the dirty little secret of the classical music world. "They shut down the feedback loop," Fanselow said. As for exposure training, it's what every mother tells her kid at one time or another. Get back on the horse, toast your brother at his wedding, play yet another recital. Has nothing changed? Psychologists have for years applied the principle of exposure therapy to treat claustrophobics, locking them in car trunks and coffins—an escape hatch at the ready. They have helped people with arachnophobia face down their fear of spiders and cajoled others with a fear of heights into glass elev- ators. Current technique relies on a gradual desensitization, beginning with mild triggers before building up little by little. So, for example, a person who is terrified of spiders will at first be exposed to pictures of spiders, before being brought face-to-face with a spider in a cage. Eventually, the spider will be let out, allowed to crawl about, and, if all goes well, be touched and petted by the arachnophobe.

This graduated exposure is used to treat yet another common and embarrassing performance anxiety. Paruresis is the inability to urinate in the presence of others, and it happens more often to men than women. Like most social phobias, shy bladder syndrome, as it is also called, derives from a fear of negative evaluation by others. But here the results can be unusually extreme. People who suffer from this syndrome will often go to great lengths to avoid urinating, even traveling across the world without visiting a bathroom. "The record appears to be three to five days, which seems way out there on the spectrum," said Steven Soifer, an expert on paruresis. He is the founder of three nonprofits (the Shy Bladder Institute, the International Paruresis Association, and the American Restroom Association), author of two self-help books, and a tireless advocate for cleaner, more private public restrooms.

Soifer works each year with hundreds of men and women. He asks them to drink copious amounts of water and then to travel from toilet to toilet. Their first field trip is usually to a hotel room, where they are assigned the job of urinating with the door closed while a buddy waits outside. Next, they work their way to a bathroom with the door open just a crack. The goal or "feared item" of choice is a large public bathroom, preferably in a casino or shopping mall. A professor of social work at the University of Memphis, Soifer traces his own lifelong problem with paruresis to junior high school, when some kids tried to break down the door of the bathroom stall in which he was sitting. "Based on all the workshops I've done, I can confidently say that the most common reason is bullying of some sort—either at school or at home, by parents or siblings," he said. "Most people who were publicly embarrassed or had some kind of trauma could develop these symptoms."

Scientists used to think of memories as photographs, their details fixed the instant they are recorded. Today, the accepted view is that memories are stored like individual files on a shelf; each time one is pulled down for viewing, it is altered or "reconsolidated," even if only minimally, before being put back in storage. Each new version sits beside the old one, like the history of a computer document that's gone through multiple revisions. They all remain in your hard drive.

Extinction training doesn't work by outright destroying a memory. Rather, it gradually defuses a memory through repeated reconsolidations. The sooner this process begins after a trauma, the greater the chance that the traumatic memory can be disrupted and pushed aside. How soon after a trauma must the process begin in order to be effective? What is the window for optimum results? In a 2007 experiment at New York University, three groups were subjected to a series of electric shocks—all administered whenever an orange square appeared on their computer screens. The fear conditioning worked; all three groups developed an aversion to the orange square. Over the next few days, researchers experimented with varying methods of extinction training to rid the subjects of their newfound fear. The first group was brought back and shown the square—shock-free—to reactivate their fearful memory. Ten minutes later, they were shown it again. Voilà! Their fear was gone. The second group was similarly reacquainted with the orange square, but didn't receive their extinction training until six hours later. The subjects in this group didn't fare as well as the first; they never did lose their fear of the orange square. Neither did the members of the third group, who were never shown the square again, never reminded of the fearful memory—and never given the chance to alter it. The experiment showed that scientists could selectively block a conditioned fear memory in humans with a behavioral manipulation. The implication was clear: Find that window—somewhere between ten minutes and six hours—and it might be possible to treat even the most intractable fears. Possibly without drugs.

The search for a chemical fix to curtail fear dates back to ancient tribes on the Siberian steppes. The shamans of the Koyak and Wiros tribes created a drug made from *Amanita muscaria*, the distinctive red-and-white mushroom commonly known as fly agaric. They discovered that when a warrior urinated after eating this mushroom, the potency of the drug in his urine was many times greater than in the mushroom alone. Warriors stored the urine and drank it on the eve of battle to give themselves courage. In time, they began feeding the mushroom to reindeer and then gathering the animal's urine, which made for an even more effective brew. It seems the compound passed unmetabolized through the reindeer's kidneys, increasing the potency still further.[6]

In North Africa in the thirteenth century, the Crusaders fought a band of Muslim warriors known as "hashshashin," so called because—as legend has it—they ingested hashish before battle to reduce fear and control pain. The English word *assassin* is reputedly derived from these hashish eaters, who made a practice of ambushing their Christian enemies. In the sixteenth century, the Incas of Peru prepared for battle against the Spaniards by chewing on coca leaves, the source of cocaine. British soldiers traditionally have been offered a double jigger of rum to steel their nerves, while Russian soldiers get vodka. During World War II, the Russians got a mild tranquilizer prepared from valerian, an herb that's long been associated with valor,[7] while the Americans and British were fed amphetamines to increase confidence and aggression and elevate morale.[8] During the war in Iraq, American troops were provided with stimulant medications including Ritalin and Adderall to boost wakefulness and learning.

Published reports have described Pentagon-funded research into smart drugs to create a fearless "supersoldier." If only such a drug had been available on London's West End when Sir Laurence Olivier confided his stage terror to the actress Dame Sybil Thorndike and her husband. "Take drugs, darling," she said. "We do."

Today's most widely prescribed drugs for anxiety—Anafranil, Ativan, BuSpar, Celexa, Effexor, Lexapro, Lyrica, Klonopin, Paxil, Prozac, Tofranil, Xanax, Zoloft—are overkill for a midlevel manager who just happens to be scared stiff about his upcoming presentation before the board of directors. That's why performers and public speakers are far more likely to dose up with a beta-blocker: "For Public Speaking" is the off-label use routinely stamped on prescription bottles. Though never approved for stage fright, the beta-blocker—usually propranolol—is the standby drug for performance anxiety.

According to one study, propranolol slightly improved the test results of medical students. Another study found that high school seniors who took it outperformed their classmates on a repeat of the SATs. But it is in music performance that the drug occupies a special niche; it's joked that an IV drip of propranolol hangs over every orchestra pit. Beta-blockers—so called because they block the heart's adrenaline-responsive beta-receptors—work by slowing nerve impulses through the heart. They make the heart pump less forcefully, lowering blood pressure and reducing demand for oxygen. They also act as a balance to the body's autonomic system, which regulates breath, heart rate, digestion, perspiration, urination, and sexual arousal.

Developed in the early 1960s, the beta-blocker was a game changer in the treatment of heart disease and one of the most significant medical advances of the twentieth century. It was the invention of Sir James Black, a Scottish doctor and pharmacologist whose father had suffered from angina and died of a heart attack following a car crash. Black sought to modulate the body's uncontrolled fear response, let loose every time the hormone epinephrine, more commonly known as adrenaline, is released. It sets off a cascade of responses: dilated blood vessels, increased respiration, and a pounding heart—all of which generate waves of anxiety and lead to more blood vessel dilation, faster respiration, and greater heart palpitation. Black envisioned a pharmaceutical umbrella that would protect the heart and cardiovascular system from this emotional rain forest of stress and fear. That's how he described it to Rein Vos, a Dutch medical philosopher who interviewed him at length in 1983 for a doctoral dissertation on the history of the drug.

Today, beta-blockers are the fifth most widely prescribed class of medicines in the United States, with 128 million prescriptions written each year as of 2009. The vast majority is for blood pressure and heart disease, but there is also a strong market for performance anxiety. Statistics are not collected for off-label usage, but it's safe to say the market is almost exclusively American. Many countries forbid doctors from engaging in the kind of off-label use of prescription drugs allowed by the U.S. Food and Drug Administration. In Japan and Holland, for example, it is all but impossible to get a prescription for "the public-speaking pill," as my own doctor called it.

Whenever I reach for my beta-blocker, I think of Alice reaching for the cake that made her larger. But beta-blockers don't make me any braver. They don't erase my anxiety. What they do is leave me with an absence of its physical manifestations. Their effect is about what *doesn't* happen. My hands don't drip with sweat. My fingers don't tremble. My knees don't shake. My heart doesn't palpitate. They deliver a negative space, something like what the Japanese call *ma*. And yet, in my mind, I never lose the familiar dread, my most intimate consort—the lump in the throat, the voice demanding to be heard, asking just what exactly I am doing and why I am so determined to do it.

I have always been the kind of person who eschewed medication, who could make a bottle of Tylenol last a decade and would rather suffer a raging case of poison oak than allow a shot of cortisone into my system. But once I started using beta-blockers in June 2012, I couldn't imagine going into a performance without them. I questioned whether my body was capable of mustering up a semblance of composure without one of the little orange pills. They were so easy to use, such a perfectly invisible crutch. Was I cheating, using them? My doctor had written me a prescription that permitted numerous refills. Dozens and dozens of little orange pills.

I told myself that I was using them strategically, to store up a new set of experiences and build up my confidence. This was my brand of exposure therapy. The new positive memories would wash away a lifetime of bad ones, and I would augment the chemical fix with a steady diet of yoga, meditation, biofeedback, and cognitive behavior therapy. In forcing my body to declare a cease-fire, they would give me the opportunity to wrest my thoughts from fear to music.

As it happens, stress reduction was one of the purposes envisaged by Black and his team of scientists at Imperial Chemical Industries in London, according to Vos, the Dutch medical philosopher. The amelioration of anxiety by propranolol was a given, and many of those scientists experimented freely on themselves, taking the pill to calm their nerves before presentations, speeches, and lectures. "I did hundreds of interviews, and many people—the top scientists in industry and academia—told me they used this drug," said Vos, a professor of theory of health sciences at Maastricht University in southern Holland. "On the one hand, they needed it. But it was also normal practice in those days [to experiment with drugs under development]."

The early experimenters consumed enormous doses—up to 3 to 4 grams at a time, Vos said. That's an astonishing amount: The standard dose for controlling blood pressure is

120 mg; performance anxiety is typically treated with a mere 10 mg. The scientists must have assumed that these were safe drugs, and compared with most medications they are. But despite their overall safety record, beta-blockers do carry long-term risks, presumably more so when they are consumed in megadoses. According to studies, 5 to 10 percent of men who take beta-blockers for heart disease develop sexual impotence. People who have severe asthma, diabetes, and certain other medical conditions are generally advised to avoid the drug, as are pregnant and breast-feeding women. It may interact with other medications. Side effects include fatigue, insomnia, disturbing dreams, cold hands and feet, and depression.

News about their magic powers spread rapidly through the medical community in the 1960s and 1970s, sparked by anecdotal reports of surgeons taking them to steady their hands in the operating room. Beta-blockers were the first performance-enhancing drug—long before the term *PED* was invented. When, in 1978 and 1982, a couple of independent studies suggested as much, they set off a storm in the performing arts world. The studies were conducted by two brothers—one, a vascular surgeon in Denver; the other, a professional organist from Towson, Maryland. The organist, Thomas Brantigan, had been searching for a remedy for stage fright all his adult life. He developed the problem as a boy performing in his teacher's piano recitals, and his anxiety had grown intractable through his years of study. When he heard about a new medication for blood pressure and heart disease, he told me his ears pricked up. "Just the word *beta-blocker*! If you can stop the beta-receptor, stop the physical response, then okay, you've solved stage fright. I did a bunch of literature searches, put together a bunch of Xeroxed studies, and went to my brother John, who's an orthopedic surgeon. He told me to get the hell out of his profession. So then I went to my brother Charles."

The elder Brantigan was intrigued. In addition to being a surgeon, he was a professional tuba player. Though he had no personal experience with stage fright, the more he researched the subject, the more he came to understand it as "a catecholamine storm," a form of "self-poisoning by adrenaline." (Catecholamines are hormones produced by the adrenal gland.) People like his little brother simply might have an overabundance of beta-receptors, he reasoned. He agreed to design a small, double-blind clinical trial, and together the brothers arranged for adjudicated performances by music students at the University of Nebraska and the Juilliard School. At each performance, half the students were given propranolol (brand name Inderal), the most commonly prescribed of all beta-blockers; the other half performed chemical-free. A portable telemetric unit monitored their physiological responses with unsurprising results: The students who got the beta-blockers had lower heart rates, lower blood pressure, and effective elimination of "the physical impediments to performance caused by stage fright." More unexpected was the verdict of three judges—a player in the New York Philharmonic Orchestra, a Juilliard faculty member, and Thomas Brantigan (who says he had no knowledge of who was given the drug). They preferred the chemically assisted performances.

The Brantigans' study was published in the journal the *Lancet* in 1978.[9] It was bolstered by their second study, conducted at the

Eastman School of Music in Rochester, New York, and published in the January 1982 issue of the *American Journal of Medicine*.[10] The response was almost immediate. In some quarters, the brothers were reviled as drug pushers, accused of using powerful medicine to treat a mere annoyance and of contributing to the end of classical music. Musicians, on the other hand, quietly began bombarding their doctors with prescription requests. By 1987, a survey by the International Conference of Symphony and Opera Musicians, which represents instrumentalists in dozens of major orchestras, revealed that 27 percent of its members used beta-blockers. Of those, 70 percent got the drug from colleagues.

But it's the rare musician who admits to it. A few years ago, Charles Brantigan was backstage with members of the Denver Symphony Orchestra when he heard a prominent player loudly condemn the practice. Anyone who can't stand the heat should get out of the kitchen, the musician declared. Brantigan was taken aback but also amused. "I had just given him a prescription for beta-blockers the day before," he said. Many musicians still quote Sara Sant'Ambrogio, cellist of the popular Eroica Trio, who in 2008 told the *New York Times*: "If you have to take a drug to do your job, then go get another job." Detractors insist that beta-blockers turn performance into a sterile and mind-numbing exercise. Angela Chan, a pianist in Montreal, told me that it made her feel like a zombie on the one occasion she tried it. "It was the most devastating experience I ever had. I became a machine to puncture all the notes. It was a total waste of time for me and for the audience. There was no music to speak of. It should be banned for musicians!"

★

Propranolol is a drug with at least nine lives, one of which holds the potential to interfere with memory formation. Neurologists at the University of California at Irvine discovered this in 1995, with a simple and very clever experiment based on the power of story. They told one group of study participants about a woman and her son who visited the boy's father at the hospital where he worked. On the way there, they saw a disaster preparedness drill featuring a simulated accident victim. The boy stayed with his father at the hospital and the mother went home. Done, end of story. The second group heard a very different account. On the way to the hospital, the boy was in a car accident in which his feet were severed. He was rushed to the hospital, where surgeons reattached his limbs, and he remained to convalesce while his mother returned home.

Two weeks after hearing these stories, both groups were tested for their recall memory. The subjects who heard the second, emotionally rousing story were able to recall many more details than those who heard the bland first story. That was no surprise. The human brain best remembers events and stories that activate the amygdala; the more emotionally activated the amygdala, the better the recall. With this in mind, the neurologists next sought to test what happens to memory formation when adrenaline is blocked. Again, they turned to narrative. This time, they told two new groups the same gruesome tale of the boy and his accident. But before hearing it, one group was given propranolol, the idea being that the drug would prevent stress hormones from activating the amygdala. The other group heard the story drug-free. While members of the first group tended to recall many of the story's details—what happened, when, and where—they didn't suffer much emotional upset. In science-speak, propranolol blocked the memory-enhancing effects of emotional arousal and stress.

Other studies followed, including one in 2010 of a Montreal man who developed symptoms of post-traumatic stress disorder after being hit on the head with the butt of a gun during a bank holdup. The incident traumatized him. He gave up his longtime hobby of bird-watching, became housebound, and broke up with his partner of many years. According to the study, the man received six treatment sessions with a psychologist: At each, he revisited the original memory after being given propranolol. By the fifth treatment, he reported that he felt unengaged when recounting the story. Two years later, he resumed his normal activities and said that although he remembered the events at the bank, he wasn't unnerved by them anymore.

Accounts like these have fired the imaginations of scriptwriters, who have portrayed propranolol as a mind-altering drug that even Aldous Huxley could never have envisaged. In 2007, the television drama *Boston Legal* aired an episode about a sixteen-year-old girl who was molested by a rabbi. Against the advice of her lawyer (who called it "the forgetting pill"), she wanted to take propranolol and put the whole thing behind her. "Why is it so difficult to understand?" she demanded. I have often wondered the same. Propranolol helps me walk the tightrope. I may not be a professional pianist, but I do know that propranolol doesn't "devastate" my playing, as it did Angela Chan's. It may not erase my negative thoughts or put me in the zone, but it dampens the adrenaline rush ("the catecholamine storm") and shuts down the feedback loop. My fear is denied its feeding frenzy, and for now I can't foresee giving up my 10 mg beta-blocker pills. And yet, what I take so casually has sunk major careers in the sporting world.

In 2008, a North Korean pistol shooter was stripped of his medals and expelled from the Olympic Village in Beijing after testing positive for propranolol. In 2009, Doug Barron became the first player in the history of golf to be suspended for doping—the dope, in this case, being testosterone and beta-blockers. Barron, who had requested a medical exemption for both drugs, sued the PGA Tour for reinstatement and returned after a year.

Beta-blockers have been listed on the World Anti-Doping Code since 2009. The International Olympic Committee, Professional Golfers Association, and National Association for Stock Car Auto Racing have, in one way or another, all joined in banning the drug. Such restrictions make sense in sports such as archery and pistol shooting, where a beta-blocker gives a distinct advantage, allowing the shooter more time to fire between heartbeats. (That is why it is classified as a performance-enhancing drug, along with anabolic steroids, peptide hormones, beta2-agonists, hormone antagonists, and other substances.) But for the rest of us, it's the drug that saves us from ourselves.

Chapter 7

MIND GAMES

THE PIANO KEYBOARD HAS always been my touch-stone, what the Soviet poet Vera Inber described, in a very different context, as "the zone of memory, where the lightest touch wounds mortally." It conjures up memories, resurrecting the past with near cinematic precision. Sometimes, playing Brahms, I pictured my mother in her late eighties, pacing up and down the length of her basement on a winter afternoon. She wasn't willing to brave the ice and snow, but she was determined to walk and would do so for a good hour, usually to the music of Brahms. Cleaning out my parents' house a few years ago, I found her boom box on the basement ironing board, and when I popped it open, there was the CD of Brahms's Piano Concerto no. 2. Other times, memories that were long forgotten would emerge full-blown. Like the time I began giggling in the middle of a dense contrapuntal Bach partita, as I remembered my uncle Benny's anger when I failed to deliver on a promise. "Sara's promises are as good as Hitler's," he burst out in a fit of pique. I was nine years old.

Random thoughts foisted themselves on me so forcefully at the piano that I occasionally arrived at the end of a piece as stupefied as a driver who can't remember the stop signs she's passed on the way home. Shut up, shut the fuck up, I told myself in the midst of some mental pilgrimage—usually while playing a sublime piece of music. I'd once read a study claiming that the average mind spawned sixty thousand thoughts per day. I hadn't tackled algebra in years, but it struck me as a classic SAT problem: If the Brahms Rhapsody in G Minor had 2,739 notes (yes, I counted), how many thoughts did I have per note? What began as a quest to overcome a fear of performance gradually transformed into a search for mindfulness. If I could maintain my focus, I might retain my equilibrium as a pianist. Nadia Boulanger, the French piano pedagogue, called absolute attentiveness a form of character. "I don't know whether attentiveness can be taught," she said. "I would say that anyone who acts without paying attention to what he is doing is wasting his life. I'd go as far as to say that life is denied by lack of attention, whether it be to cleaning windows or trying to write a masterpiece."[1]

Mindfulness became yet another skill to practice while I was practicing. I decided that the next time I noticed my thoughts drifting to the past, I would leave the piano and pull out a box of old family photos. I hadn't gone back to the piano to commune with the ancestors and explore my childhood. I wasn't practicing four or five hours a day as a substitute for journaling. This was supposed to be about striving for excellence. Now, when I sat down, I tried to home in on the touch of my fingers on the keys, my sitting bones on the bench, my feet on the floor. I posted notes all over the music: "BREATHE!" The messages reminded me of a friend and her daughter, who bore the same tattooed word on their right wrists. Breathe! Why does it require a reminder? Every emotion alters the breath, one way or another. But when we're scared, we seek to deny or ignore our fear, and holding our breath becomes a physical tool of that denial. Breathing— so autonomic, so much a function of the reptilian brain—is easy to forget. Sometimes, as I played, I realized that my chest wasn't moving, my diaphragm was still, my throat stuck between an inhale and an exhale.

In the spring of 2012, I heard about a biofeedback program called BodyWave that was designed to measure brain waves during periods of concentration. The nuclear power industry, NASA, NASCAR racing teams, and the U.S. Women's Bobsled National Team all used it to improve performance. In the case of the bobsledding team, a 3D simulation was designed to allow the athletes to strap on the BodyWave and practice-drive a bobsled down a twisting, turning course. "If they started to lose their attention, the sled would start to shimmy and tip over," reported Peter Freer, founder and CEO of Freer Logic, the company that makes the device. "We immediately knew who the 'green' drivers were. They were the ones talking to themselves, thinking, Oh no! Watch out! The veteran drivers are able to pull themselves back. Even though some fear is always there, they are able to recover in a fraction of a second. And that's because there's an incredible amount of correlation between thought and fear. The more you speak to yourself, the more fear and less success you get."

When I wondered if the device would be useful as a way of measuring my focus at the piano, the company sent me one to try out. It was the size of an iPhone. I strapped it to my ankle with a strip of Velcro and ran a cable to my laptop perched on top of the piano. The device would monitor my brain activity as the computer's camera recorded me playing the Bach Prelude and Fugue in C Minor. Telling myself that this was a test, I immersed myself in the playing. I concentrated. I banished all other thoughts but Bach. So I was shocked when I stopped the program and looked at the results. The graph of my brain waves looked like an EEG (electroencephalogram) of someone who was having a heart attack. The lines jumped up and down without apparent pattern. During passages in which I was convinced I had been in deep concentration, the waves plummeted, revealing a sharp decline in focus.

The program also came with a computer game. To play, you were supposed to focus on a lotus flower and watch the petals open. As soon as you lost focus, the petals closed. It looked simple, but no matter how many times I tried, I couldn't open the flower all the way. I would make it halfway before it closed up again. I stared it down, emptied my mind, breathed in and out, and willed the petals apart. I observed my breath. I felt my eyes widen with the effort. I decided the game was loaded. A friend who had practiced Tibetan Buddhism for many years offered to take a look. She strapped on the BodyWave and within a minute willed the lotus open.

Amy Beddoe was a nursing professor who had written her doctoral dissertation on the use of mindfulness and yoga to control pain, stress, and insomnia during pregnancy. She had studied with Jon Kabat-Zinn, the Boston molecular biologist who brought meditation and mindfulness training to mainstream medicine. Beddoe had offered many times to teach me how to meditate, and I'd always shrugged it off. This time, I took her up on it. As we settled ourselves on the floor of her living room, she told me that meditating was like taking a little vacation from thinking. I didn't have to regulate my breath or do anything to control it. All I had to do was watch the breath. She set the timer for half an hour and we sat companionably, eyes closed, until the buzzer went off. Okay, I thought. Good. Kind of relaxing. I tried the next day, accompanied by my big smelly dog, Zella, who acted as if she were getting quality time. She plopped herself beside me, let out a long sigh, and breathed with an equanimity I tried to emulate. I reminded myself of Beddoe's words: I was taking a vacation. But after maybe five minutes, it occurred to me that I really liked thinking and didn't enjoy being on vacation so long. It looked easy, but it was hard. Every afternoon that first week, I sat on the floor thinking about all the things I might be doing instead. Practicing. Walking Zella. Picking weeds. Calling the bank to protest a fee. I was sure I could get it reversed. Breathe, I told myself. It was such an easy thing to forget. It wasn't as if my body were going to forget to do it.

I had been taking yoga classes for a couple of years at my gym, trying to concentrate over the whirr of treadmills and stationary bikes and a teacher who ended every class with a pseudo–New Age off-key chant that made me grit my teeth, though I was supposed to be in a deep and relaxed state of Shavasana, or

Corpse Pose. I was ready to quit when Amy Beddoe told me about her yoga teacher. Kofi Busia had studied with B. K. S. Iyengar, founder of the most widely practiced form of hatha yoga in the world; Busia was one of the few teachers ever awarded a senior certificate by Iyengar. Though his classes were never advertised, they were packed, mostly with students who had been coming to him ever since he moved to California from England twenty-two years earlier. From the moment I walked in I felt a gravitational pull, enhanced by the calming sound of Busia's voice as he circled the room, dressed (always) in a heavy cardigan sweater and sweatpants, stepping between the mats and limbs of thirty or more people, mostly but not all women.

It had been an improbable path that brought Busia to California. He was born in a small village in Ghana, the son of an Ashanti prince who was the first member of his tribe to read and write. His father, Kofi Abrefa Busia, was elected prime minister of Ghana in 1969. Three years later, his right-of-center government was driven out of power in a military coup. The family fled the country and went into political exile. Kofi, my teacher, was eight years old at the time. He spent the rest of his childhood in England, attending a public boarding school before winning a place at Oxford University. Trained as a classical pianist, he practiced seven to ten hours a day. At Oxford, he became interested in yoga. What started out as a whim became increasingly serious, until he stopped practicing the piano and traveled to Pune, India, where for the next six years he studied off and on with the master, his guru, "Mr. Iyengar." During that same period of time, he studied for his doctorate in medical anthropology from Oxford.

Kofi Busia

An often enigmatic teacher, Busia communicates in meta-phors, anecdotes, and stories. One of his favorite subjects is focus, but when he talks about it, it's often filtered through the lens of philosophy, biology, music, poetry, or anatomy. It's always a surprise, what Busia riffs on. I remember one class where he spoke about rivers for nearly two hours. He touched on the rivers of North America, Africa, and Asia, describing in detail how they wound through the land, complemented the topography, and linked up, one to the next. I gradually began to observe my body differently, how it flowed, where it clogged, and where the muscle linked to bone. Once in a great while, Busia chants from one of the *Yoga Sutras of Patanjali*, which he has translated from the Sanskrit. And while the class is often grueling, to the point that I sometimes ache for assistance, he rarely adjusts his students. According to him, each body will, given the opportunity, find its way. When he does offer an adjustment—tweaking a leg to improve balance, pulling back an arm to open the chest, pressing down on a back to extend the spine—it is with the understanding that something in the body has begun to shift. It is less a correction of something wrong than an affirmation of progress. We, his acolytes, see intention in almost everything he says and does. When, during one of his forays around the room, he bumps against the ankle of a student in Reverse Triangle Pose, she assumes he is conveying something essential about her posture. When he makes a joke during Shoulder Stand, we conjecture that his attempt to make us laugh is intended as a way of forcing air through our diaphragms and that with this greater breath we will lift ourselves higher off the floor.

After four years of attending Busia's classes, I have become a convert. Yoga has improved my life. My balance is better. A test for bone loss no longer indicates osteoporosis in my right hip. I am sleeping deeply for the first time in years. In the months leading up to my recital, I realize that my focus even seems to be improving at the piano. In yoga class, I have stopped stealing glances at the clock; sometimes, I forget to count the seconds (or minutes) that Busia has left us in Shoulder Stand. "Concentration is contentment," he offers up, urging us, as always, to create more space inside our bodies and our minds. "Concentration moves through the body, creating quietness, balance, and poise," he intones. When he defines focus—"the marshaling of all one's faculties to accomplish a goal"—I try to bolt the words inside my mind. But sometimes I don't listen at all. The sound of his voice and the mood he fosters are enough to create a focal point, one that allows me to home in on the endless details of a pose.

At the piano, my thoughts, posture, gestures, and music making all require a yoga mind. But my attention, so assiduously cultivated and hard-won in the yoga studio, doesn't automatically transfer to the piano, where that union of mind, body, and instrument still proves elusive. Frederic Chiu, a pianist renowned for his piano transcriptions, addresses this problem in his workshops for advanced pianists. He often leads them at his manor house on a Connecticut estate dotted with shady old-growth trees and modern art installations. His workshops draw on ancient philosophy, meditation, and "aspects of music making usually left uncovered in traditional study." But the issue of stage fright is always forefront. Chiu considers it a universal response to performing, whether the musician acknowledges it or not. For him, it comes down to shame and humiliation.

"The more interested and excited about something you are, the more intense your shame and humiliation will be when the passion gets stopped," he explains. "And it will always be stopped by something, at least some of the time." By a mistake. Or by a momentary loss of focus. To inculcate attentiveness, Chiu has created what he calls "stop exercises." During a piece, an exercise, or even a scale, the musician must regularly stop playing and ask himself, "What am I experiencing emotionally right now?" Of course, the answer will always be different, depending on the moment and the music. "The more observant one is, the more one is watching, fully aware of what's happening and of what might happen. The more you peel away these added layers of affect to get at the core, the more you see."

It is a form of meditation at the piano, a way of stopping and paying attention to the press of the fingers, the resilience in the wrists, and maybe the ache in the shoulders.

Richard Davidson, a University of Wisconsin–Madison neuroscientist and lifelong meditator, preaches an almost evangelical belief in the plasticity of the human brain at every stage of life. He has come to this conclusion in part through his research on the transformative brain waves of lifelong meditators: Tibetan Buddhist monks. "The amazing fact is that through mental activity alone we can intentionally change our own brains," he writes in *The Emotional Life of Your Brain*, coauthored with science writer Sharon Begley. "Mental activity, ranging from meditation to cognitive-behavior therapy, can alter brain function in specific circuits, with the result that you can develop a broader awareness of social signals, a deeper sensitivity to your own feelings and bodily sensations, and a more consistently positive outlook. In short, through mental training you can alter your patterns of brain activity and the very structure of your brain in a way that will change your Emotional Style and improve your life."[2]

Meditation lowers anxiety by enhancing the circuitry between the left prefrontal cortex and the amygdala. It turns out that the prefrontal cortex, the logical, analytical part of the brain, the region most associated with executive function and higher thinking, is also associated—on the left side—with positive emotion. The more active the left prefrontal cortex, the more resilient—or, as Davidson puts it, Resilient—one is. This understanding has been confirmed by dozens of studies and MRIs that show the more activation there is between the left prefrontal cortex and the amygdala, the more emotionally resilient the person is. But the range of variation among individuals is staggering. The amount of activation in the left prefrontal region of a Resilient person can be thirty times that of someone who is not Resilient.

How resilient am I? Based on my history at the piano, it would appear that the answer is "not very." Definitely a small *r.* In my worst moments, I worry that my hippocampus, that little seahorse in the brain, may be a bit shriveled. It is well-known that chronic stress can impair the function of the hippocampus, which plays a critical role in consolidating short-term memory into long-term memory. (After a fear memory is laid down in the amygdala, it gets consolidated in the hippocampus.) Research has shown that people whose post-traumatic stress disorder is caused by repeated trauma (soldiers exposed to severe and repeated carnage in combat, individuals repeatedly abused as children) have smaller hippocampi. But there is also intriguing evidence for a chicken-or-egg dilemma, that having a small hippocampus may actually precede the PTSD and thus predispose one to the disorder.

It may seem frivolous and even presumptuous to compare a case of performance anxiety with PTSD, but in fact a 2012 study of orchestra musicians in Australia did just that. The study found that 33 percent of the musicians met the criteria for a diagnosis of social phobia, while 22 percent identified themselves in a questionnaire as positive for post-traumatic stress disorder. The author of the study, psychologist Dianna Kenny, concluded that detailed memories of mangled concerts were recalled with "a clarity and emotional 'present-ness' that resemble, in some instances, the flashbacks experienced by those who suffer post-traumatic stress disorder."[3]

Damage to the hippocampus interferes with a person's sensitivity to context. The soldier who patrols the streets of war-torn Tikrit on high alert is doing his job. When he brings that same hypervigilance home to the States, he is undone; the sound of a car backfiring puts him over the edge. Post-traumatic stress disorder is a disorder of disrupted context. A damaged hippocampus—unable to form memories of the context in which a trauma occurs—inhibits the ability to distinguish the screech of an incoming bomb from the siren of a fire truck. Luckily, the brain's plasticity can help compensate. In his book, which reads like part science, part self-help, Davidson writes that "thought alone can increase or decrease activity in specific brain circuits that underlie psychological illness." The extent of such neuroplasticity is evident from MRI studies of people who were born deaf. Their auditory cortex, the part of the brain ordinarily reserved for hearing function, is appropriated for peripheral vision. "It is as if," Davidson writes, "the auditory cortex, tired of enforced inactivity as a result of receiving no signals from the ears, took upon itself a regimen of job retraining, so that it now processes visual signals."[4]

Correspondingly, people who are blind from birth and who learn to read Braille show a measurable increase in the size and activity of those parts of the brain ordinarily reserved for visual function. "Their visual cortex—which is supposedly hard-wired to process signals from the eye and turn them into visual images—undertakes a radical career change and takes on the job of processing sensations from the fingers rather than input from the eyes."[5] It's not such a great leap, then, to assert (as Davidson does) that a person can modify his or her brain through meditation. The practice of mindfulness trains one to redirect thoughts and feelings—"the manifestation of which is nothing but electrical impulses racing down the brain's neurons." Mindfulness practice strengthens the left prefrontal cortex at the expense of the right, a nifty exchange given that the right prefrontal cortex is usually predominant in depressed people. Fifty years ago, Timothy Leary counseled a generation to "turn on, tune in, drop out." Davidson's message goes like this: "Breathe deeply, stay focused, change your brain."

Meditation is a way to take stock, observe, and create distance from the obsessive internal chatter. A psychologist at the University of California at Berkeley is exploring another tool to calm the mind, with a simple experiment that engages the kind of self-talk more typically associated with preschoolers. Ozlem Ayduk asks university students to recount a personal experience by using the third-person voice, shifting from "I" to "he" or "she." The shift from first person to third appears to dilute the emotion that is otherwise inflamed by the recol-lection of a distressful experience. It alters perception and allows the mind to create some distance from the experience. The meaning of that memory may then be reinterpreted and its negative association resolved. Not unlike meditation, it allows the individual to adopt a more compassionate response to his or her own failings.

It's the difference between this: *What an asshole I am. I can't do anything right. I never play the piano the way I want to play. I should just give up and quit.*

And this: *Poor Sara! Why is she so scared? When she made a mistake during the Brahms rhapsody, how did she feel? Why does she get so upset when she makes a little mistake? Why does she think she has to be perfect?*

The UC Berkeley students in Ayduk's 2014 study were ordered to deliver an impromptu speech and perform a series of math tests, counting backward by threes and sevens—all in front of a panel of evaluators instructed to correct their every mistake and judge their intelligence. "It basically makes people completely freak out," Ayduk says, grinning. Physiological measurements confirmed it: The students' stress levels soared through the roof. But the students who reflected on their feelings in the third person showed less stress, reported less shame, and scored higher in the math drills.

"People who use the first-person pronoun are really just rehashing what happened," Ayduk explains. "They tell a story by saying, 'First this happened, then I said this, my boyfriend said that, and then I said . . .' That's the way autobiographic memories are encoded. It's about the sequence of events: where it happened, who was involved, what was said and done, what emotions were felt. People taking the third-person perspective also do that. We all do that." Yet the students who told their stories in the third person were able to make peace with an experience and walk away from it. The meaning of the story had changed. It was reinterpreted and released as a source of stress. One of Ayduk's colleagues, Jason Moser, a psychologist at Michigan State University, conducted EEG studies that found a dramatic change in brain waves between first- and third-pronoun usages. Students were wired up and exposed to a series of images, some neutral, some gruesome. The neutral images included a coffee mug, a tissue box, and a light bulb. The gruesome images were truly gruesome: a mutilated body, a woman held at knifepoint, a shark attack. The students were asked first to reflect on their responses to the images in the first-person voice. During the second round, they were asked to reflect while using their first names.

"In the first person, when they used the word *I*, we got the normal brain response," reports Moser. "It lit up for the emotional scenes. But when they used their own names, moving into the third person, the emotional response pretty much went away. And it happened within seconds."

The approach bears comparison with mindfulness practice in that it teaches people to stand back and observe their emotions, thoughts, and behaviors in a healthy way. As Fritz Perls once said, attention "in and of itself is curative." The practice of meditation demands that one observe every thought, every sensation, every feeling, without judgment. *My concert is only six months away and I already feel scared. I just don't know if I can do it. Hmm, interesting that this thought has entered my brain.* Or we can try to lessen the amygdala response by talking to ourselves in the third person. *Sara has had some difficult performances in the past and now she's scared that she may never get her act together. She forgets that she is very prepared and doesn't have anything to worry about.*

I have been multitasking ever since I was a little girl, propping the latest Nancy Drew mystery on the music stand while executing Hanon exercises in every key. Now, occasionally, at the end of a long and demanding yoga class, I find myself in Shavasana, in a state of unfettered thought and judgment. The space around my body feels extended. I float untethered. It is a moment of sublime concentration. The instant I grasp for it, it eludes. More often, I am thinking about what I plan to make for dinner, which of my kids I'll call on the way home, and how much more piano practice I want to get in before I climb into bed. The lights are off, thirty bodies lie prostate all around me, and I'm still multitasking. How do you change a habit to which every part of your body reverberates? One way is to just keep coming back to the breath.

Chapter 8

ME AND MY SHADOW

D ENNY ZEITLIN'S EARLIEST MEMORIES are of climbing onto his parents' laps and placing his little hands over their big ones as they played the piano. The family's Steinway grand dominated the living room, and when Zeitlin was two or three he was given free rein to explore it, to clamber around inside, crawl over the soundboard and across its steel wire strings, to pluck them and lose himself in an ecstasy of sound and touch. Hours went by like this, he remembers, during which he struck and clanged the strings with spoons and blocks and other household objects, before moving on to the black and white keys. It was permission, he says, with a capital P.

Zeitlin is proof that an unhappy childhood is not a prerequisite for becoming an artist. The San Francisco–based jazz pianist and psychiatrist grew up in a Chicago suburb, with an older sister and two doting parents. His father was a doctor, his mother a speech pathologist, and both were amateur musicians. At seventy-five, Zeitlin is still drawn to those "intergalactic sounds" from childhood, still exploring and creating sound worlds that challenge orthodox assumptions of what constitutes music.

With more than thirty-five albums under his belt, Zeitlin is a musician's musician who twice placed first in the DownBeat International Jazz Critics Poll. He has composed music for *Sesame Street*, and he scored the 1978 remake of *Invasion of the Body Snatchers*. He also is a clinical professor at the University of California at San Francisco, where he teaches psychiatric residents, and has a full-time private practice in San Francisco and Marin County. A lanky, bearded man, he runs up and down Mount Tamalpais, not far from his home in Marin, at least four days a week and is an expert fly fisherman who travels to Christmas Island in the central Pacific for bonefish. Though he has never experienced serious stage fright ("The first time I played Newport Jazz in '64, I looked out and there were ten or fifteen thousand people; I was a little nervous"), he has come to understand it.

Music has always been his main portal to a state that he calls "merging." His first such association—the toddler almost becoming one with his parents—was soon followed by others. He remembers as a child waking up early and going downstairs to play the piano, eventually noticing, out of the corner of his eye, that his mother had followed him down and was sitting and watching, quietly listening, refraining from comment. Her presence floated across the room to join his, generating a force that spurred him on in some unidentifiable but pleasurable way.

When Zeitlin speaks about the merger state, he means the dissolution of individual boundaries, a spontaneous

Denny Zeitlin (Courtesy of Josephine Zeitlin)

transformation of becoming part and parcel of everything and everyone around him. Merging is a way of taking on different aspects of the world and becoming whole with it. On the bandstand, it is triggered when he loses himself in the music and experiences a synesthesia of sounds, where the notes have tastes, textures, and colors, and B, for example, is purple, A is red, D is yellow, and F is green blue. "When I begin to get those experiences, it's a signal for me that I'm on the verge of entering that merger state." Musicians and athletes call it "the zone"—a place where the music seems to happen independently of the player.

Music is still the primary portal. ("When I play my best, I often have no idea who's creating music. I'm aware there's music happening, but I am not aware I'm playing the keyboard. I could just as easily be playing the drums.") But it's not the only one. There are many kinds of mergings: physical, emotional, spiritual, and sexual. When running in the mountains near his home in Marin County, he finds himself flooded with sensation, merged with the wind, light, and landscape. A related feeling comes upon him at the office when, as a psychiatrist, he enters into a profound sense of understanding with the person sitting in the chair across from him. "There is a tremendous commonality between improvising music and working with patients on a deep level," he says. "It's entering into a merger experience at its most intense, where the boundaries dissolve out of choice, and yet a part of oneself remains available to observe and comment on the process. In the office, the patient is the protagonist and I'm the accompanist. It's analogous to what I do as a pianist when a trumpet player takes a solo. How can I support the story this person is trying to tell? How can I try to enhance it or give it some meaning?"

At the age of six, Zeitlin requested classical piano lessons. He progressed quickly, showing such talent that by the time he turned ten, his piano teacher told his parents it was time to start grooming him for a concert career. He needed to devote himself to a lot less socializing, a lot more practice. "My parents said no, our son is the one who's going to decide where music is going to take him, and I am so grateful to them for that. I never would have been happy as a classical pianist, playing the same notes over and over, interpreting what someone else wrote on a page. I was always impatient. I would learn a piece of music, and once I understood how it was put together, my interest in performing it was nil. What I was interested in was how that material might infuse my improvisations and compositions."

When he was fourteen, he was introduced to the piano music of George Shearing. Zeitlin had never heard jazz before, but as he listened to the ten-inch LP with a photograph of the blind pianist on the cover, it hit him "like a blitzkrieg. The first piece I heard was his version of 'Summertime,' and I was knocked out by that. The way he used classical technique to make new music. It had drive, it had propulsion, and they were making up some of it as they went along!"

By age fifteen, he was driving—with his parents' blessings and the key to the family car—to the South Side of Chicago, where he hung out ("the only white kid in a black club") with some of the era's leading jazz musicians. It was education by osmosis, absorbing the work of pianists such as Chris Anderson (who would also become a mentor to Herbie Hancock) and Ahmad Jamal (an inspiration to Miles Davis), eventually sitting in with major players such as saxophonist Johnny Griffin and trumpeter Ira Sullivan. There were nights that Zeitlin didn't get home until four.

His love of music was rivaled only by a fascination with psychiatry. He first learned about it from his Uncle Howard, a psychoanalyst who regaled the boy with stories about his work and the people he met. The idea that other people had inner lives enthralled Zeitlin and gave him a whole other window on life. When he was seven, he emulated his uncle in the schoolyard, setting up a table at recess where classmates could come and discuss their problems. From an early age, he was convinced he would be involved in both fields. Years later, the pianist Billy Taylor, another important mentor, urged him on toward medical studies, telling him that a musician's life on the road was not an easy one; better to keep it as an art form, not a means of making a living.

His psychiatric approach was shaped by his long association with the psychoanalyst Joseph Weiss, a leading theorist of modern psychiatry. Once a week for thirty years, until Weiss's death in 2004, Zeitlin "bought consultation," meeting him at his San Francisco office to discuss theory and research and to brainstorm how to help his patients. "It was the outstanding educational experience of my life," Zeitlin says. "He turned my work around. I never before had such a clear idea of how psychotherapy worked, and soon I found that I was making enormous progress with my patients." Weiss formulated an influential theory that negative "pathogenic beliefs" about oneself and relationships with others arise from childhood—sometimes from traumatic events, but most often from long-simmering dysfunctional family dynamics. These beliefs lead to psychiatric symptoms and maladaptive behaviors that are doomed to be repeated in future relationships unless the patient can find the key to change. Unlike Freud, who in his early writings promulgated the idea that people exert no control over their unconscious mental life and actually obtain gratification from their neuroses, Weiss argued that patients exercise considerable control over their unconscious processes and have a wish to overcome their problems. He called his approach "control-mastery theory." According to the model, the therapist's role is to serve as an ally and help the patient follow her unconscious "plan," to disprove her pathogenic beliefs by acquiring insight and "testing" the therapist. Zeitlin calls it "a cognitive, relational, humanistic theory," because, he says, everyone has an unconscious plan for how to rid themselves of their pathogenic beliefs.

A case early in his psychiatric career gave him an opportunity to test that theory. "A jazz saxophone player—I'm thoroughly disguising this example—came to me because he felt he played wonderfully in rehearsal, but as soon as he stood in front of an audience his performance would fall apart. He was a superior player. He brought in tapes of his music so I could hear it. It seemed like a clear case of fear of failure. He had always gotten top grades in school, been popular—a real golden boy. The possibility that he could not get up in front of an audience was devastating to him.

"As I understood his family dynamics, his younger brother was not so nearly blessed. He didn't get the good grades, he didn't have the musical talent, he didn't have many friends. As we explored that, he remembered incidents of his brother's unhappiness. He felt guilty that his life had gone better, that at times he enjoyed feeling superior to his brother. Yet he also worried about him. He had a pathogenic belief that the assets in a family must be parceled out equally. He dealt with his 'survivor guilt' by holding himself back in his music to somehow level himself with his brother." The more Zeitlin explored the family history, the clearer it became that his patient was experiencing the same survivor guilt toward his band mates. "As we worked through it, he began to play more and more in public and began feeling joy in kicking ass and even allowing himself to feel superior to his fellow musicians. They 'passed the test' by responding very positively, helping him to disconfirm his pathogenic belief that everyone had to be equal in ability. It was an extremely therapeutic experience. He'd been the lame one in the band, and now he was the star."

Zeitlin became known as an expert in the creative process. As his psychiatric practice grew, it attracted a large number of artists, particularly performing artists. Many came because they were experiencing creative blocks. "Most of these people had heard I was a performer and hoped I would understand their experience. And certainly performance anxiety has come up a lot. I try to discover what pathogenic beliefs are producing this symptom, and there are numerous possibilities. Often, guilt over success can masquerade as a fear of failure, as in the example of my 'saxophonist' patient. It's an underappreciated theme in psychotherapy, and I've found it very valuable to tune in to that. It happens when someone doesn't feel they deserve to be successful. They snatch defeat from the jaws of success. They'll convince themselves they're really impostors."

Most performers who admit to stage fright trace it to childhood. It's always easy to blame one's parents. But when it comes to classical music, ballet, equestrianism—anything that demands early exposure, dedicated practice, and excellence— the parental voice lodges itself deep and early, as intertwined in the child's psyche as the strands of the double helix. I once met a middle-aged violinist who told me that the instant she pulled the bow across the strings, she didn't hear music; she heard her father's censorial voice. I had gone looking for the psychological underpinnings of my own stage fright, reaching out not only to Zeitlin, but to Freudians, Adlerians, Jungians, and integrative psychologists and psychiatrists. Their insights were provocative and sometimes helpful, but they didn't necessarily guarantee my own progress. When it came down to it, this was *my* fight.

Unlike the Zeitlin living room in suburban Chicago, where a Steinway grand doubled as an indoor playground, the modest Heintzman upright in the Solovitch house in Port Colborne, Ontario, was downright fetishized. When I was a little girl, my mother looked on as I washed my hands, then inspected them on both sides before I was allowed to sit down and play. If I didn't get down to business right away, I was accused of banging, or "boompking." Even today, the idea that a child would be allowed to clamber over and around a soundboard strikes me as crazy.

I was encouraged to merge with the piano in other ways. One of my earliest memories is of lying under my aunt's grand piano, feeling my body reverberate to the sounds and vibrations of that enormous beast. When I came up for air, it was to watch my aunty Maddy's hands fly across the keys. I can still remember thinking how odd it was that the notes rang clear even as her fingers fogged up in a blur of motion. Aunty Maddy had begun studying the piano when she was three years old, taking lessons from a pianist her mother had known in Russia. Madam B. came to my grandparents' walk-up in Syracuse and introduced Maddy to the piano with the C scale: "One, two, three, pass the tomba," she dictated in a thick accent. When the little girl, with her chubby fingers, failed to execute the scale and turn her thumb properly, Madame B. became infuriated, threw her into a closet, and locked the door—fighting off my grandmother's pleas to let her baby out. Abusive as that was, it had no lasting impact on my aunt's love of music. She played Chopin especially beautifully, attacking the études and mazurkas and ballades with passion. Her hands probably weren't much larger than mine, but in my memory they spanned the keyboard. Her playing conveyed uncomplicated joy; even when the music was sad or pensive, she played as though she were thrilled to be alive.

As a pianist, I was her opposite, controlled by the shadow, what Carl Jung called "the inferior part of the personality." He meant, of course, the unconscious, which has to be recognized and assimilated for a whole, integrated self to emerge. Jung knew all about the fear of public speaking, defining it as an illness of the consciousness of the self. "What can one say to a person who is self-conscious?" he said in a series of seminars called Visions. "You cannot be better than you are, why should you be self-conscious? You are just foolish. I have to say the same thing to myself, too, of course, and I know very well why I need it. Everybody is sick for a time with that self-conscious business."[1] It is in that collection of seminars that Jung tells the apocryphal story of a tongue-tied Alcibiades, fearful of speaking before the people of Athens. Classicists and scholars of ancient Greece say they can find no evidence of the tale in the historical record and question whether, Jung created it as a way of explaining, perhaps even taming, his own fear.

In classic Jungian thought, stage fright is a primal fear, awakening archetypal memories of ourselves as herd animals thrust outside the safety of the pack. Our predators—the lions, the sharks, the audience—smell our vulnerability and hover nearby, waiting for that one mistake.

"To make one's self conspicuous is to detach one's self from the herd, to stand apart and alone," wrote Dorsha Hayes, an actress and dancer who, after a bout of rheumatic fever ended her performing career in 1936, became a poet, novelist, and essayist on Jungian psychology. In an article titled "The Archetypal Nature of Stage Fright," she analyzed the dread of poets who read their verse in public. "In our long human history, severance from the group has always held an element of danger, and we may assume that a behavioral pattern has been formed and is deeply imbedded below the level of consciousness . . . Down through the centuries, the one who stood alone was vulnerable and helpless against the massed attack of his fellows; he was the outcast, the victim, the one who could be lynched, tortured, stoned to death, crucified. Man's fear of man is causal in origin. It is the individual who has known the inhumanity of man."[2] The archetype of the stoned man or outcast, embedded in unconscious memory, is, in Hayes's words, countered by the image of the leader who has led his people to clear water, the one who "can walk safely among the many for as long as his counsel serves the general good." The unconscious image of the stoned man underlies the fear of every individual who steps out onstage alone.

John Beebe, a Jungian analyst who lectures internationally, told me he used to suffer deep anxiety from public speaking. "I was standing up there, quite literally trying to perform to a group of people with very high standards. And I had imagined that I was like a bride before her wedding and that I could not see the groom. As though I were pure and virginal and white. I decided that image was all wrong. So what I began doing was, when I came into an auditorium, I would go up to people I knew and shake their hands. It surprised people. They don't expect you to do that. But by affirming them like that, when I got up onstage I felt I was speaking to people I already had a rapport with. Now I do that all the time and it comes very naturally."

We were sitting in his San Francisco office, the same small, brick-walled room he has maintained since opening his practice forty-five years ago. Beebe is a film buff who has written widely on the power of cinema to illustrate ideas of the shadow: "the thing a person has no wish to be," as Jung put it. He is especially drawn to the archetype of integrity, which he sees as a dialectic between persona, the face we present before the world, and anima, or soul. This tug and pull between showmanship and sincerity implicitly shapes the way we respond to performances. The great ones are explorations of honesty, searches for truth.

Beebe threw a leg over the arm of his chair. The actor and singer Liza Minnelli, he said, was a case in point. In 2011, she gave a comeback performance at the Royal Albert Hall in London. As Beebe began to describe it, he grew so animated that he stopped the conversation, drew himself straight up in the chair, and turned to his computer. Yes, there it was, a YouTube clip of Minnelli singing "But the World Goes 'Round." She was her usual ebullient self, glamorous in purple sequins, holding tight to the microphone and belting out the words with vaudeville intensity. When Minnelli came to the part about broken dreams not mattering, she sang,

Take it from me, there's still gonna be
A summer, a winter, a spring and a fall

I was aware of her overly wide vibrato and cracked notes; it was the voice of an aging performer. Minnelli struggled a few minutes and came to an abrupt halt. She turned to face the band and muttered something about the second verse. Either she had just lost her place or she wasn't happy with her singing. She wanted to go back and fix it. The pianist groaned but started again, a few bars before where they'd left off. This was her signature song, the one she made famous in the 1977 movie *New York, New York*, and now that she was sixty-five, the words sounded as if they were about her.

She started up again, and—though far from perfect—her performance came right from the gut. "Sometimes your heart breaks," she sang, and it was all there: the hardships, the triumphs, the years of alcoholism and drug abuse. She knew it, and the crowd knew she knew it. A roar tore through the audience. "Did you hear that?" Beebe demanded. "That was more real, more electrifying, than any perfect performance. What was always scary about Liza to me in the past was that she was so perfect. Here, she's working the dialectic between persona and anima. It gives her performance integrity."

Beebe urged me to consider a little-known Jungian theory, "a lovely, lovely theory," known as "deintegrative anxiety." It is a model of child development that begins in infancy and describes how the self is built, one experience at a time. It happens every time a baby surrenders her self or "wholeness" and opens up to another. She takes her first tentative steps toward her parents: That is deintegration. They catch her with open arms, and she understands that she is loved and supported: That is reintegration. According to this theory, life is an ongoing cycle of deintegration and reintegration, a constant flux between breakdown and assimilation. Every time we open ourselves to someone or something new, we risk giving up a part of ourselves. A healthy self will deintegrate and reintegrate continually throughout life. Any change to the status quo represents a threat to the whole, but most of us assume some degree of risk and adventure, knowing that our lives will be more interesting and fulfilling for doing so. If we're lucky and survive these risks, we will integrate them into our selves.

Consider making performance an experience of reintegration, Beebe advised me now, pointing out that no one who has performed has ever failed to experience some deintegration. The important piece in this is to factor in imperfection. "There is something about trying to be perfect that lacks integrity," he said. "When you present yourself honestly, it's hard for someone to knock you off, because you never pretended in the first place to be perfect. It's about a mix of confidence and unconfidence—that's much safer. It's bulletproof. Liza Minnelli, she can't break down because she's already broken down. She's aware that one can break down, and there's a durability to that."

It was now January 2013. I had begun inviting small groups of friends and acquaintances over for a series of Saturday evening recitals. I called them soirees, but I thought of them as my personal, custom-designed form of exposure therapy. These were small gatherings of six to eight people, with ample opportunity for deintegration and reintegration. The idea was that I would play through two or three of my pieces, after which we would retire for wine and dessert. I believed that these kind people were humoring me or at the very least doing me a favor, so I was taken aback when they actually seemed to enjoy themselves. They had questions: Why was I doing this? What had gotten me started? What did it mean to go deep into the music? And what was I learning about myself? They often entreated me to play some more, especially when I botched a piece. Play it again, they said. Inevitably, I played better the second time.

The first few soirees were exciting but exhausting. I usually took a beta-blocker an hour before my guests arrived, and I worried that it would wear off if they came late or dawdled before I played. I found the act of performance to be draining and often couldn't wait for everyone to leave. Afterward, I couldn't fall asleep. I suspected the beta-blocker caused my insomnia, but I didn't dare play without it. How many mistakes had I made? How badly had I played? Beebe might call it deintegration and reintegration, but I felt caught in a school-yard game of Red Light, Green Light; for every two steps forward, another two steps back. How many of these deintegrations and reintegrations would I have the stomach to undergo?

But after three or four of these soirees, a shift occurred. I began playing more fluidly and confidently. I was making progress. At one gathering in April, I began with the Bach

Prelude and Fugue in C Minor and moved on to the Brahms Romanze in F Major, and I found myself enjoying it. I decided to keep going. My little audience's response was so enthusiastic when it was over that I felt I had given them something valuable. Time was running out. But with two months remaining before my big recital, I was beginning to see possibilities beyond my own internal struggles.

The most famous child prodigy of the twentieth century had an upbringing full of deintegrative and reintegrative experiences. Two hours after Ruth Slenczynska's birth on January 15, 1925, her father, Josef, a Polish violinist, examined her wrists and hands in the hospital nursery in Sacramento, California, and between sobs of joy declared she had the makings of a great musician. "Look at those good sturdy wrists!" he proclaimed. "Notice the way her thumb is separate from the rest of the hand! Look at the tips of her fingers! I swear to you, Mamma, that's a musician!"[3]

In her memoir, Slenczynska recounts the ruthless training that turned her into a wunderkind. It began when she was three, banging away on a toy piano while her father, a self-taught violinist ("He was not a great musician. He couldn't count. And counting is not that hard"), gave lessons in an adjoining room. By the time she was four, Slenczynska was practicing nine hours a day, every day of the week. No mistake went unpunished. A missed note was met with a whack across her cheek, and if the mistake was especially egregious, she was hurled from the piano. Her father boxed her ears, swore at her in five languages, and pulled her shoes off in wild rages. On the one occasion her mother reached out to protect her, Ruth screamed at her, "Daddy's right! Stay out of this! It's none of your business!"[4] Every new piece began with a threat: "Let's see if you can learn this without a wallop." It is almost without irony that she writes of the great progress she made under her father's heavy hand. "I am ashamed to admit that until I was fourteen years old, and had already been on the concert stage for ten years, the only new piece I ever learned without a slap was the first movement of Schumann's Piano Concerto. For some reason, I showed immediate affinity for that music, learning it in perhaps three hours. I felt completely secure with it that very first time I played it, and Father, tough critic that he was, paid me the compliment, for once, of keeping his hands to himself."[5]

She hated her father yet lived for his approval. He dictated every minute of her day, from the time she woke up and began practicing (six A.M.) to the way she parted her hair and what she wore when she practiced (a petticoat, so as not to ruin her dress with perspiration). When she was four years old and preparing for her first solo recital at Mills College in Oakland, she asked him what would happen if she made a mistake. He went into the kitchen, returned with half a tomato, and threw it in her face. "That's what will happen," he answered.[6]

When she was six, the family moved to Europe so she could study with some of the most legendary pianists of the day: Sergei Rachmaninoff (who called her the greatest talent he had ever heard), Josef Hofmann, Alfred Cortot, Artur Schnabel. She made her debut in Berlin that same year. Three years later, when she performed in Copenhagen, she was examined by two medical specialists after newspapers in that city suggested that she was a dwarf; in their opinion, no child of nine could play as she did. At the age of ten, she replaced the Polish pianist Ignace Paderewski, after he suffered a heart attack and canceled his scheduled performance at Carnegie Hall. With only a few days' notice, she stepped in to play his exact program. For her first encore, she performed Mozart's Sonata in F Major; for her second, Chopin's Étude in A Minor (the *Chromatic*). When it was over, Ossip Gabrilowitsch (a Russian-born pianist who was married to singer Clara Clemens, Mark Twain's daughter) turned to a fellow pianist and said, "I worked on that piece twenty-five years before I dared to play it in public. I'm sure she hasn't put quite that much time on it."[7]

As Slenczynska entered her teen years, however, little "buts" began to creep into the reviews of her performances. The word *immature* was frequently applied. Her obedience and slavish practice—at times exceeding eleven hours a day— failed to produce the acclaim she had come to expect as a child prodigy. "It was as if each time that terrible word appeared in a review, I was branded anew. It made me feel condemned, tainted . . . The inferiority complex it gave me was frightful. I began to think I was not made for music, that there was something glaringly wrong somewhere, so wrong that none of my teachers, least of all Father, could correct it."[8]

Slenczynska's memoir has been out of print in the United States for decades. In China, however, it is in its third print-ing, studied as a primer for music education, its eighty-eight-

Child prodigy Ruth Slenczynska at eight years old (Ruth Slenczynska Collection, Lovejoy Library, Southern Illinois University Edwardsville)

year-old author regularly sought out for advice. "Wherever I go, Chinese people seek me out. They want reassurance from me that it's possible for their little kid to be made to work and become extraordinary like me. And it is." What she doesn't tell them is that there is no such thing as a natural prodigy. "It's the most manufactured process you can imagine. Just like a rose is highly cultivated. Or a prized tomato. Or a prized pig."

The first time I talked to Slenczynska on the phone, she was generous with her advice about how to practice ("I don't allow my students to play scales two-handed"), memorize ("Accept that you are stupid and don't know anything and therefore play the right hand alone, working on a passage

that's no more than four bars long"), and prepare for the inev-
itable stage fright ("Ordinary calisthenics—it gets the blood
moving, the blood goes to your head, and you feel good").

I was delighted when she invited me to visit her the next
time I came to New York. I arrived at her apartment, not far
from Lincoln Center, a couple of hours before she was scheduled to teach a lesson, and she greeted me, a short woman in a
knit suit. Her living room was dominated by side-by-side
Steinway grand pianos, with a bank of windows overlooking
the Hudson River. There was little empty wall space; most of
it was covered with oil paintings, Chinese prints, and litho-
graphs; a discreet corner held a collection of photographs and
personally signed thank-you notes from Presidents Truman,
Kennedy, and Reagan.

"I think he'd be actually surprised to see this apartment,"
she said, glancing around her with satisfaction, referring back,
as always, to Father. I asked if she ever felt a twinge of gratitude toward him. By her own account, she would have had a
very different life if he hadn't driven her so hard. Wasn't there
some irony in the fact that the man who nearly destroyed her
was also responsible for the life she enjoyed today? "That's
only because I had the courage to run away," she snapped.
"He beat me. When his hands weren't enough, it was 'the
magic stick.' When the stick wasn't enough, it became his
belt. No girl likes that, to run around the house being chased."

I mulled that over, remembering how my own mother
used to chase me around the dining room table, flailing a
wooden cooking spoon, half yelling, half laughing, at me to
practice. In my memory, it looked like a game of tag—far

from the abuse meted out by Slenczynska's father. But I also wondered what made him so effective.

Other people apparently wondered the same. No less a pianist and pedagogue than Artur Schnabel, the Austrian pianist renowned for his Beethoven interpretations, once asked Josef Slenczynska for child-rearing advice. "How did you start her?" he demanded, according to Slenczynska's memoir. "I took my own son as a little boy and locked him in a room for eight hours a day and I made him study all by himself. That boy is sixteen and he is a young man now, but he can't do what this little child of yours is doing. What did you do with her?" "That boy"—Karl Ulrich Schnabel— would in fact go on to have a fine career as a pianist and teacher, with a special interest in the literature of four-hand piano music.

As I said my good-byes to Slenczynska, she told me about one of her few remaining students, an eleven-year-old boy who was giving small recitals around New York. He had recently asked her the same question she'd once posed to her father. What would happen if he made a mistake at an upcoming recital? She smiled, crinkled her eyes, and answered in her kindliest, gentlest manner: "Your mother will still love you and I'll still love you. The only difference is that people who were thinking of you as excellent will think of you as just okay." She was her father's daughter.

Susan Raeburn, a clinical psychologist in Berkeley, California, suggested that I carried unresolved intergenerational loss, by which she meant that I was burdened by the ghosts of previ-

ous generations, alert and responsive to the wishes and expectations of people long dead. I regularly thought about my
mother, father, and aunt and almost unconsciously consulted
them before making any important decision. But did that
mean I was carrying unresolved grief and trauma? I felt deeply
beholden to my aunt, whom, as a child, I always pictured with
a fairy wand in hand. She was the one who bought me my
first piano, sent me to summer camp, funded my college
education, and showered me with gifts and opportunities I
never otherwise would have known. I believed that my
mother felt so beholden to her older sister that when I was
sixteen she offered me up as a sacrifice. She relocated our
family from a little town in Canada to an even littler town
three hours away in upstate New York. And when she realized that she had made a mistake and moved the family back
again after a year, I stayed behind to finish high school and
assume a life apart. My mother's sense of duty splintered our
family and changed my life. Jungians would probably see it as
a modern-day version of Rapunzel, the story of a young girl
handed over at adolescence to an older enchantress.

"Whatever doesn't get resolved in one generation gets
unconsciously carried into the next generation," said Raeburn,
who grew up in a musical family ruined by alcohol. Her
father was Boyd Raeburn, the big band leader of the 1940s and
1950s. Her mother, Ginnie Powell, was a jazz vocalist who
toured with Gene Krupa and had a voice that was sometimes
compared to Ella Fitzgerald's. Her mother died when Raeburn
was eight, her father when she was fifteen. Though there had
always been lots of partying and drinking, it was years before

she recognized the role alcohol played in their lives. Later, she would write her doctoral dissertation on the subject of stress in the world of rock musicians, and a big part of her present-day practice centers on helping them overcome addictions.

An integrative psychologist, she draws on different schools of thought, from psychoanalytic psychotherapy to Jungian depth psychology, cognitive behavioral and dialectical behavior therapy, and mindfulness. She draws inspiration from the work of John Bowlby, the British psychiatrist whose theory on the primacy of attachment between mother and infant is back in vogue after years of neglect. Bowlby's work in the second half of the twentieth century picked up where Freud left off: All anxiety is separation anxiety. Despite the distance that modern psychology has traveled since Freud, separation from the mother is still widely seen as the root of all anxiety. In Freudian terms, stage fright represents a reversion to infantile behavior, rooted in the unconscious and beyond conscious control.

"If the mother is drunk, anxious, or depressed and doesn't accurately pick up on the child's signals, the child will learn a confused way of understanding his own experience," Raeburn said. "If the parent isn't attuned enough of the time—because nobody is a perfect parent—the child grows up having to adapt himself to the parent. The child is so out of touch with his own needs, he's taking care of the mother and doesn't recognize his own experience."

It wasn't a clear parallel to my own experience, but I suspected she was talking about me. Raeburn speculated that my performance anxiety served an important, maybe even restorative, function. It was my body's protest against something I was otherwise powerless to protest. If as an adolescent I couldn't refuse my mother's expectations and stop entering those endless competitions, my body would speak up on my behalf. It gave me an out. As Raeburn described it, performance anxiety became my ally. I somatized my anxiety, put it squarely in my body. Her advice now: Make the piano mine, not my mother's. I was not a concert pianist and never would be. My status did not depend on it. Find a relationship with the music that is all yours, she urged. I no longer needed the piano—if I ever did—to prove my lovability or worth. Instead of trying to fulfill my mother's expectations, I had to come back to music on my own terms. Only then would my stage fright go away.

Chapter 9

SO MUCH FOR PERFECTION

A MID PREPARATIONS FOR MY performance, I was offered a cautionary tale by a pianist who had been blinded by the pursuit of perfection. John Orlando was a well-known figure in my town, the former chair of the piano department at our local community college. He was a generous man who donated the lion's share of his mother's inheritance to a community foundation for a Yamaha concert grand. A respected teacher and mentor, he was also a presenter of concerts by emerging pianists from around the world. Music was his life.

Orlando recently had given a concert with a chamber orchestra, hired at his own expense, at a hall that he had rented and for which he personally sold 152 tickets. At seventy-one, he was determined that the show be perfect, that people see and hear him as the musician he really was. He had given many concerts throughout his life, but he always was haunted by insecurity. He dated it to his childhood.

The son of a San Jose farmer, Orlando grew up hating the family farm. Every calamity that could befall a farmer befell his father: A tractor toppled over on him, a horse kicked him in the mouth, a hay hook pierced his hand, he was poisoned by agrochemicals. John Orlando determined from an early age that his life would be different.

His first instrument was the accordion, which he began playing as a seven-year-old. He progressed quickly, learning the standard tunes that his parents loved. His teacher composed music just for him, and he was soon an up-and-coming talent in the Italian American community of San Jose, performing in regional competitions and on local TV shows. Then he discovered the piano, and it was as if he'd discovered ambrosia. He would never touch the accordion again. He got his first piano when he was fourteen, but it was not until four years later—when he enrolled at San Jose State College as a music major—that he had his first lesson. Eighteen years old is late in life to set one's sights on becoming a professional pianist, but nobody told Orlando that. If they had, it wouldn't have stopped him. Every morning for the next four years, he snuck into the college music building before the doors opened, to begin practicing at six thirty. He stayed until ten at night, resenting even the fifteen minutes it took to run and grab a quick lunch. He practiced so much that his shoulders seized and his arms became muscle-bound; he sometimes had to play eight hours just to loosen up. For years after graduation, he traveled to New York to study at an institute for injured pianists. There were periods when he stopped playing repertoire to focus on his technique, overhauling it to reach the point where he could play without pain.

Even beyond the physical pain, his big hurdle was stage fright. Over the years, he tried numerous remedies, including

EMDR, shorthand for Eye Movement Desensitization and Reprocessing. As the therapist moved her fingers back and forth in front of his face, he followed her motions with his eyes and recalled "the vessel of fear" that seemed to encapsulate him as soon as he walked onstage. He remembered the memory lapses, the mistakes, and the pangs of shame and humiliation. He learned to replace traumatic memories with good ones, and it seemed to help. After a series of treatments, he gave a performance of which he was proud. But his fear was capricious; it came and went. He never knew when it would seize him. Once, backstage, he made a small joke that made the stagehands laugh and gave him confidence as he strode to the piano. He played brilliantly, he told me, and naturally attributed his triumph to the joke. But when he reached for levity a second time, the joke fell flat and his stage fright only deepened. There were performances during which the keys felt strange beneath his fingers and he was consumed by distracting thoughts—chief among them that the audience suspected he was faking his heartfelt connection with the music. "I would think about the phrase I was about to play and remember that I'd screwed up in the past. So I screwed it up again. To overcome it, I tried harder and became more tense. I pressed into the keys, which created more resistance from the instrument. That can create a false sense of expression. You look like you're feeling something, but it's like being exposed and trying to hide at the same time."

In his late sixties, he suspected his fears were being stoked by his new career as concert presenter, introducing superb young musicians to audiences on the central California coast.

It was all his doing, and the job gave him tremendous satisfaction. The young players were so talented, so perfect. "I wanted to be like them," Orlando said. "I was driven toward perfection. I was obsessed with it."

The pursuit of perfection dogged him as he prepared for his concert in March 2012. In the months leading up to it, he practiced with his usual zeal. He retained a performance coach, read seven books about peak performance, and listened to every available recording of the Mozart Piano Concerto no. 15 in B-flat Major, the piece that he would be playing. Orlando compared his own playing with every one of the recordings; in everything he heard, there was the ideal and then there was him. Though he had had memory lapses in the past, he insisted on performing without the music. ("It's a crutch. As if I don't know the music!") He categorically refused to consider taking a beta-blocker ("Never!"), and when a friend suggested he go for a walk and get some sleep, he resented the advice.

"I was hell-bent on my own destruction," he later said. "So caught up in trying to be perfect that I was blinded. I knew the music inside and out. I practiced twelve to fourteen hours a day for months before the concert. I was obsessing about little details right up to the last day. There are certain people whose nature is more vulnerable, and I probably fall into that category. My parents were both filled with anxiety and there was tremendous tension between them, much of it unacknowledged. I'm still particularly aware of that unspoken feeling, that you can't ever know what's going on.

"Some people feel entitled to success," he continued. "I never felt I deserved it, I think because I was angry at my parents.

Failing became a way for me to get back at them, a way of wanting to be accepted for myself alone. I didn't want to have to prove anything [to an audience], to have to pay a price for being accepted. As a result, I was willing to sabotage my performances." He seemed to be saying that the love of the audience had replaced his parents' love and it still wasn't enough. He was seeking unconditional love. "Because the acceptance and adulation I would get wasn't what I really wanted. By failing, I wanted to be accepted for myself. What other people thought was very prominent in my mind. Unusually important to me."

He was a man of contradictions—one minute doubtful that he was deserving of success, the next convinced of his excellence as a performer. He demanded that the audience see and hear him as the pianist he knew he was, and if it meant "getting back in the ring" to be knocked around, he wouldn't hesitate.

Orlando hardly slept the week before the concert, choosing to practice nearly twenty hours a day. The night before, he sat up and meditated. He was exhausted before the performance began, and once it did the problems emerged almost immediately, when he made a premature entrance into the music. The orchestra easily covered it up. Orlando had chosen to perform what many regard as the most difficult of Mozart's twenty-seven concertos. Even the composer, writing to his father in 1784, had called it a piece that would make a pianist sweat. Still, Orlando appeared largely in control until the first cadenza, a lengthy solo passage that begins sparely, with every elegant note and phrase exposed, and then gives way to a rush of scales and trills that would challenge the most accomplished of virtuosos. Amid these cascades, he suffered a memory slip and had to start again. There was another memory slip in the second movement, and then, a little while later, it happened again. By the third movement, Orlando was rattled. This time, when he came in two bars early, the conductor waved her baton to stop the music. After a long pause, she counted aloud and the performance resumed. By the time Orlando got to the end, many in the audience felt almost as drained and anxious as he. Leaving the hall, some people privately wondered why he chose to put himself through so much pain.

I thought of my own concert, now two months away, and what my guests—some flying from across the country—would think about me. Would I make them cringe? Would they resent me for subjecting them to my slips and stumbles? I

John Orlando (Courtesy of R. R. Jones)

thought about what my friend Paul, a bit of an elitist, once said, that anyone who can't manage to play without errors shouldn't perform. And I asked myself if I was being a fool. What, exactly, was I setting myself, and my friends, up for?

Recovering perfectionists often quote Tolstoy's maxim that "if you look for perfection, you will never be satisfied." But as a youth, Tolstoy was himself quite the perfectionist. At eighteen, he began a Journal of Daily Activities in which he set forth a list of rules for developing his willpower and improving his character. Every evening, he laid out the next day's schedule, dictating exactly how many hours he would dedicate to study, leisure, meals: Wake at five A.M. Eat in moderation. Avoid sweet foods. Walk an hour every day. Do only one thing at a time. Visit a brothel no more than twice a month. Ah, rules to live by! By old age, he had renounced his perfectionist tendencies: "To reform all humanity and eradicate all human vice and unhappiness seemed plausible enough to us at the time, just as it seemed an easy and uncomplicated matter to reform ourselves, to master all virtues and be happy," he wrote. "God alone knows, however, just how absurd those noble dreams of youth were . . ."

Around the same time in the late 1840s, such "noble dreams" led John Humphrey Noyes—American socialist, zealot, and coiner of the phrase *free love*—to found a utopian society in Oneida, New York. The Oneida Perfectionists, as they called themselves, sought to establish a prototype for Jesus's perfect millennial kingdom. Their version of this paradise combined communism and open marriage—the marrying of all the men to all the women. Monogamous relationships were virtually banned; the elimination of jealousy was one of the first steps on the path to perfection. Noyes also designed meticulous experiments in "human stirpiculture"—better known as eugenics—for the breeding of better children. But the cornerstone of the ideology was the institution of Criticism. For the Perfectionists of Oneida, Criticism was the "main instrument of government . . . useful as a means of eliminating uncongenial elements, and also to train those who remain into harmony with the general system and order," according to one 1875 account. When a member of the community was sick in bed, his fellow members would gather around and treat him to the "Criticism-cure." They chastised one patient, who was bedridden for months with a spinal infection, chills, and fever, for being a hypochondriac who was overly concerned with his own health. One of his critics opined that he seemed to know a little too much about his own physiology and that "as he uses it, it is really a hindrance to him: he knows too much about his case."[1]

Criticism was the vitamin C of Perfectionism. "Many cures were attributed to this treatment," recounted Pierrepont Noyes, son of the founder, in his extraordinarily odd memoir describing everyday life among the Perfectionists. "It is even claimed that criticism and cracked ice ended an epidemic of diphtheria after all other remedies had failed."[2]

In 1879, the elder Noyes fled to Canada to escape sex crime charges, and the community's couples soon broke off into monogamous pairs. The utopia was finished when the remaining Perfectionists split their collective wealth and regrouped as a silverware company.

Ballet, classical music, gymnastics, and equestrianism are disciplines whose demands appear tailor-made for perfectionists. They exact years of training, practice, and blistering self-evaluation—the very principles that perfectionists live by. No one can attain mastery in any discipline without a relentless drive for excellence. But the line between excellence and perfection is a thin one, and a body of research shows that it's the people most preoccupied with perfection who are most vulnerable in performance. Canadian psychologists Paul Hewitt and Gordon Flett point to "a perfectionism paradox" that requires athletes to achieve perfect performances even as the traits of a perfectionist personality subvert the very act of performance. Because, as John Orlando can tell you, there are two audiences at every performance. The first audience is external, the other is internal. They may witness the same event, but they don't hear the same music, watch the same play, take in the same speech, or follow the same sporting event. For the perfectionist, the internal audience is the one that terrifies. It is ruthless and unforgiving, seizing upon every misstep, punishing the performer for every error, repudiating an entire performance for a blemish that no one else has registered. The accomplishments pale next to the failures. As with Caesar, the good is interred with the bones.

Hewitt and Flett argue that *nothing* good can ever come of perfectionism, which they define as a neurosis, implicated in depression, eating disorders, even suicide. They illustrate their argument with the story of "Mr. C.," a fifty-year-old writer whose life unraveled after he discovered a single error in one of his published works. He was a lifetime perfectionist who regarded himself as never being "quite good enough in any of his pursuits." After he discovered his mistake, his confidence declined, his writing grew disorganized, his career faltered, and he was fired from his job. Always a loner, he distanced himself from others more than ever. Unable to bring himself to inform his wife that he had lost his job, he began drinking heavily and finally tried to kill himself. Later coaxed into counseling, he brought along a copy of his résumé so that the therapist could "get to know him quickly."[3]

"Mr. C." brings to mind the French celebrity chef Bernard Loiseau, who in 2003 shot himself in the head when he learned he was about to lose his perfect three-star Michelin rating. An official from the guide had recently paid a visit to Loiseau's famous restaurant, La Côte d'Or, to express concerns about its irregularity and "lack of soul." As Loiseau—a manic-depressive who at the time of his suicide faced a mountain of debt—once said, *"C'est jamais gagné."* The battle's never won.

The perfectionist equates a perfect performance with self-worth, an impaired performance with worthlessness. This love-hate is at the crux of Jennifer Sey's memoir, *Chalked Up.* The 1986 National Gymnastics Champion, Sey was one of the sport's golden girls—that is, until she wrote her blistering exposé detailing the years of withering criticism and twice daily weigh-ins required to reach her goals. She acknowledged that she was born with a competitive streak and a "near manic ambition" that gave her a willingness to endure punishing hard work, a diet of fruit and laxatives, and a host of injuries, including the breaking of her femur, the largest, strongest bone in the human body. But she also laid blame on an overzealous mother (who threatened to boycott her high school graduation if Sey quit gymnastics) and the trainers at her win-at-any-cost gymnastics club in Allentown, Pennsylvania. "I can see the fat on you!" one trainer berated her. "Can you see yourself? After all this. All we've done. You're gonna give it all away. You're nothing!"[4]

Research on dancers, gymnasts, figure skaters, and high divers links perfectionism to high rates of injuries. "Most of the injuries, far and away, are overuse injuries," says Bonnie Robson, a Toronto psychiatrist who has worked with Canada's National Ballet School and other dance companies throughout North America. "You know that old joke? How do you get to Carnegie Hall? Practice, practice, practice. Well, doctors will tell you that the way to ruin your career is practice, practice, practice." Robson's research has found that 47 percent of dance students suffer a chronic injury by the time they reach high school.[5] Among professional dancers, that figure hovers at 66 percent.

The perfectionism common among dancers has long been attributed to a tradition of harsh teaching styles. Early training, a desire to prove oneself, and a focus on the teacher's approval create a confluence of negative effects. Now, at least, the culture of secrecy is changing, according to Robson, who's a specialist in performing arts medicine. "Before, when it came to anxiety or even injury—you would whisper, 'Oh, so-and-so is injured.' And the implication was that the injury was her fault. Her technique wasn't correct; she didn't have strong technique. No wonder. When the fact was that she was probably injured because her teacher was driving her on. But if you asked the teachers, they'd say, 'Oh no, my dancers don't have injuries.'"

In one study of perfectionism in sports, athletes who scored high in "concern over mistakes" reported that images of their mistakes ruled their thoughts during competitions; the study implicated poor attention and increased stress levels. Another study looked at the high incidence of hip injuries in young dancers and gymnasts. It pointed to stress and perfectionism as causation and suggested "an overemphasis on 'concern for mistakes'" by teachers and coaches.[6] Additional studies have found a direct link between perfectionism and injury—specifically focal dystonia—among classical musicians, who are expected to adhere strictly to the written score and never to make a mistake. Focal dystonia is a neurological condition that can affect the hands of pianists and string players, causing the fingers to curl— hence the nickname "pianist's cramp." A 2005 study in Germany predicted that one in every one hundred musicians will develop the condition, which also cramps the embouchures of wind and brass players. Almost all of them will be men who suffer from anxiety disorders and perfectionistic thinking.

Leon Fleisher, Gary Graffman, and Glenn Gould are among the best-known pianists who have been affected by focal dystonia, and it is now thought to be the problem that ended Robert Schumann's concertizing aspirations. The Romantic composer was a legendary neurotic; as a young man, he blushed and stammered while reciting his poetry to friends, developed unrequited crushes on young men and women alike, and suffered a terror of rejection. He was a born pianist, but after his father died he agreed to enroll in law school to placate his pragmatic mother. There, instead of attending classes, he practiced the piano up to seven hours a day. Perhaps that's where his physical setbacks began. He was twenty-one when the middle finger of his right hand, the *digitus obscenus*, went numb. He tried various self-help cures, including the use of a homemade chiroplast, a fiendish finger-stretching device popular with music students of the nineteenth century. In his diaries, Schumann referred to it as his cigar box. He rigged up a sling that was attached to the piano to hold his immobile finger aloft while allowing the other fingers to play away. These efforts did more damage than good, and soon he was turning to even more extreme remedies, such as electric shocks and animal baths. The latter involved slaughtering a live animal (a calf, pig, or lamb), into whose hot entrails Schumann would plunge his afflicted finger. It was a common cure of the age; the intestinal blood and feces were thought to have healing powers.

Throughout these self-ministrations, his future wife, the young Clara Wieck, was off touring Europe with her father (who also happened to be Schumann's piano teacher). It was her first major concert tour, the one that would begin her ascent as the most famous pianist of the age. One can imagine the obsessive practicing that Schumann—in love with the virtuoso daughter of his teacher—entered into as he prepared for the Wiecks' homecoming party. He was expected to perform his *Papillons*, a suite he'd composed in 1831, for the returning heroes, but by now his fingers—the problem appears to have spread—were almost paralyzed. So one can also imagine the relief Schumann might have allowed himself to feel. Now, at least, he had an excuse not to compete against Clara for piano primacy—a good thing, too, as he surely would have lost.

★

Nancy Shainberg Colier is a New York psychotherapist who has treated dozens of actors, dancers, singers, musicians, athletes, and writers for stage fright. In almost all cases, she found that their fear was driven by a self-inflicted demand for perfection. Colier defined perfectionism as "a gilded cage, a trap," and it was one she knew intimately. For as much as she deplored it, she questioned whether she would ever have become a top-ranked equestrian, competing on the national horse show circuit for twenty-five years, if she hadn't been a perfectionist. She grew up in a family of New York intellectuals and spiritual seekers. Her father, David Shainberg, was a psychiatrist who with his friend and fellow seeker, the physicist David Bohm, traveled around the country making a series of films with the philosopher Jiddu Krishnamurti. Her mother, Diane Shainberg, was a psychologist and Tibetan Buddhist nun whose writings helped pioneer the integration of Western psychological precepts and Eastern spiritual practices. Throughout the 1970s, the Shainbergs' Manhattan brownstone was the setting for a series of spiritual "dialogue groups," delving into the mysteries of the collective unconscious. The breakfast table was a place for dream interpretations, where children and adults were encouraged to remember and recount their nightly visions.

"There was a way that whatever you were doing belonged to the family," recalled Colier. "You were expected to bring something to the table: 'What have you got?' That was the attitude. My parents were such big presences.

"So I found a place—horses—that could not have been more different from their world. The horses were an opportunity to be somebody growing up in this family. Riding and winning became an opportunity for self-definition. And it was something that could bypass the mind, which I think I was looking for. The trainers were almost military, which appealed to me. It was really hard, there were no excuses, there were edges. In my family, in psychology, there's something soupy. There's nothing soupy about horses; there's a toughness that really appealed to me."

Colier is a slender, agile woman whose physique is of someone half her age but whose weathered complexion reflects a lifetime spent outdoors. Throughout her twenties, while working as a writer and producer in Manhattan for *Good Morning America* and *The Geraldo Rivera Show*, she drove out to Long Island every day before dawn, arriving at the stables at four A.M. to put in eight solid jumps before reporting to her

Nancy Shainberg Colier in 2001 equestrian exhibition (Courtesy of Teresa Ramsay)

job back in the city. She thrived on the detail and precision of horsemanship—what it signified, for instance, when a horse shifts its weight a few pounds to the left as it canters to a jump. She worked with a trainer who could detect, as she rode past him at forty miles an hour, that her right thumb needed adjustment. If she would just tweak it by half a millimeter, no more, the horse would hold his head differently, his neck would relax, and she would take the jump more efficiently.

"You think about the hours," Colier mused. "Ten thousand hours? That's like the first month. When I see that number, I laugh." She was referring to *Outliers: The Story of Success*, the popular book by Malcolm Gladwell, in which he repeatedly cited the ten-thousand-hour rule. The key to mastering any discipline, he wrote, was putting in roughly ten thousand hours of practice. One of his main examples was a study by psychologists of young violinists at the Berlin Academy of Music. While all of them had begun playing at about five years of age, their practice times began to diverge after a few years, so that by age twenty, the elite performers each had averaged more than ten thousand hours of practice. The merely "good" violinists logged in at about eight thousand.

Elite performers don't just work harder, however. They focus better. And at some point, they fall in love with practice to the extent that they don't want to do anything else. That's what happened to Colier. "It's that no-matter-whatness, that you can't imagine life any other way. There is no better feeling in the world than to take a horse around for eight perfect jumps, to have a horse rise up into you and lift up its knees and drop its head and climb up almost like a spider into you . . . It fills your body. It's breathtaking, and when you finish that and everything gels, it's the perfect storm. It can keep you fulfilled for months."

That was the positive aspect of what kept her going. There was also the negative perfectionist part that made her ruminate on every one of her mistakes, like a criminal returning to the scene of a crime. Had she closed her outside leg coming out of that last turn? Had she moved up to the jump too quickly? Had she lost her sense of presence? The errors would torment her. She would play them out for weeks after a less than perfect competition.

If her horse spooked at the rustle of a windswept candy wrapper, she could move on. Horses can be high-anxiety creatures, ever sensitive to their riders. In the equine world, it's a given that a horse can feel, see, and hear your fear. Colier could always forgive the horse. It was when the error was of her own making that she couldn't forgive. Equestrians are known to be "supreme perfectionists," given to flaunting "that fierceness, that toughness," expected of riders. "There's a certain level of expectation we have of ourselves," Colier said. "Perfectionism comes out of a great need to say something about who you are fundamentally. When we make mistakes, we're not the person we need to be . . . But yes, I do think it makes you better. Yes, it does make you not accept mediocrity. So it is good for that . . . It makes you better, it makes you show up more. But the suffering that goes into that is extreme. What I put myself through, that level of self-attack, it's very painful. There's no *no* with perfectionists. You are not allowed any excuses. If you didn't sleep the night before, if you're sick—nothing applies to you."

Colier never completely banished the perfectionist within, but she managed to find some compassion for her suffering and sadness. Now, when she works with Olympic hopefuls, she tells them with authority that being afraid to make mistakes actually creates mistakes. If you can't try new things, you can't get better. If you can't get better, you can't become great. An obsession with perfection stunts growth.

One of the most freeing statements I heard about perfection-ism came from Gwendolyn Mok, a pianist who has performed on the BBC and in many of the world's leading concert halls, both in recital and as a soloist with major orchestras, including London's Philharmonia Orchestra. In 2002, she made an acclaimed recording of Ravel's complete piano works.

In June 2013, I drove up to Berkeley to play for her. It was just a couple of months before my own concert, and I wanted her feedback on the way I was approaching Debussy's *Reflets dans l'eau*. It had presented a challenge to my technical abilit-ies, with its liquid surges and waterfalls of notes. I was just beginning to feel comfortable with the piece and hoped she might have some insight. "The worst thing that anyone can do in a concert is play accurately," she said right away, surprising me. "It's boring as all hell." Mok wasn't advocating sloppy playing; she was referring to the broader concept of mastery, an umbrella word that encompasses dynamics, phrasing, gesture, meaning. I was too intent on playing the right notes, she said. I was supposed to be "playing water," but my hand gestures were too stiff. They needed to be more balletic, to mirror the reflectiveness and liquid flow of water. If perfection was the goal, she said, a computer could be programmed to play the notes, rhythms, and dynamics of the piece.

She remembered a concert she had seen many years ago, given by two elderly musicians, the violinist Zoltán Székely and the cellist Gabor Magyar. They had made their names as young men with the legendary Hungarian String Quartet. The night Mok saw them, they performed a Brahms piano trio with a pianist, "and they couldn't play as well as they used to. But every note, gesture, and phrase was loaded with meaning. They were so determined to communicate that you soon forgot that, intonation-wise, it wasn't perfect, that they couldn't do some of the technical stuff. By the end of that concert everyone was in tears. I'll never forget it. To me, that was the beginning of my understanding that playing note-perfect was not the goal."

I had lashed myself to the image of a note-perfect performance. That was still my goal when I drove out to Ron Thompson's farmhouse in Montpelier, Vermont, one afternoon. Thompson was a serial careerist, an unprepossessing Renaissance man who began his professional life as a Juilliard-trained classical trumpet player when, in 1961, at age nineteen, he joined the National Symphony Orchestra. He later quit music to become an electrical engineer, then changed careers again when he was fifty, becoming an Adlerian psychologist. He knew all about the self-inflicted wounds of perfectionism; they ran like an extra chromosome through his family line. He grew up with a grandmother who was fluent in twelve languages and called the local radio station to correct the announcer if he mispronounced a word.

When he was a young trumpet player, Thompson's method was to beat himself into perfection and then practice some more. Even after three seasons with the National Symphony, he still suffered stage fright. It turned his saliva into a dry, ropy substance that dulled the vibrations between lips and mouthpiece, distorting his embouchure. Like all trumpet players, he had his tricks: Biting into a jalapeño pepper or a lemon before a performance usually did the job. But there is no such thing as a quiet mistake on the trumpet. The performance schedule of the National Symphony was grueling—about two hundred concerts a season—and the pressure was unrelenting. Six hundred performances and he still had stage fright? He blamed his nerves on the audience. He hated "the goddamn audience."

Ron Thompson (Patricia Lyon-Surrey, Fine Art Photography)

Sometime later, during a performance with the Santa Barbara (California) Symphony, Thompson had a chance to look at the audience from a different angle. The orchestra was playing the Ralph Vaughan Williams Cello Concerto, which is scored without trumpets. Thompson wandered up to the balcony of the Old Mission Santa Barbara, where he looked down on the audience he so despised. What he saw was a sea of gray-haired patrons, half-asleep and snoring in their chairs. "This audience I was looking at bore *no* resemblance to the audience I was thinking of from my first trumpet chair. There was one older man, I'll never forget him, who was taking care of his disabled son. And I asked myself, Who is the real audience? The real audience is within me."

Create your own audience, he urged me now. Take it with you wherever you play. Love yourself into excellence by cultivating an internal audience that's loving. I had been sitting at his dining room table for hours, long finished with the Caesar salad that he and his wife, Maggie, had set down for me. They were vegans, and though he insisted that they loved to cheat, they didn't cheat that afternoon. While I ate chicken, they nibbled on tofu. "Don't get stuck on perfection," he cautioned. "There is no such thing. In masterful performing, you understand the presence of error, and what you do first is learn from error and—right from the beginning—forgive the error."

It took Thompson years to learn that lesson. As a professional musician, he had disclaimed any and all error; in his mind, there was no room for a mistake. When he became an engineer, however, he learned that while a product had to be manufactured for the greatest possible precision, it nevertheless had to be designed for error or, as it is known in engineering, tolerance. In his work as an electrical engineer, he supervised and monitored the production of high-speed generator flywheels. The design tolerances were microscopic: 30 microns, or 30 millionths of a meter. "You design for errors. You always acknowledge for error, but you go for excellence. There's no such thing as perfection—in all systems. In the real world, there's always errors, always shortcomings."

Thompson quoted his friend and mentor, Charlie Schlueter, the former principal trumpet with the Boston Symphony Orchestra, who chortled over having once missed a low C— the easiest note on the trumpet—in front of some five thousand people at the Tanglewood Music Festival. "I had to fight the urge to slap my knee and laugh out loud," Schlueter told him. "It's the funniest damn thing that ever happened to me."

That, said Thompson, is playfulness. "You absolutely forgive yourself for every error—because you absolutely know there's going to be another. That frees a person to take a risk." He paused. "How else can I help you?"

By now, the sun was setting over the Green Mountains. Thompson brought me into his living room, where three trumpets were sitting on their stands. He picked up the smallest of the three, a piccolo trumpet, and began playing from Johannes Prentzel's Sonata no. 75 for trumpet, bassoon, and basso continuo. His cheeks reddened as he stood before me, playing the baroque cadenza, a whirl of spiraling melodies that shot past at flywheel speed. It wasn't perfect, but it was breathtaking. Thompson wasn't a perfectionist. He was an artist.

Chapter 10

UM . . . UM . . .

MARTHA GUTIERREZ, AS I'LL call her, is the kind of person who reads an e-mail five times before clicking the send button. A self-described perfectionist, she is not just good at everything she tries her hand at; she's the best. When she discovered that she wasn't able to speak in public, she could hardly believe it. It happened in her first semester of law school, when she was in the middle of presenting an argument against the death penalty. One minute, she was glancing down at a document, preparing to make her next cogent point. The next, she looked up, noticed six of her fellow students peering in through a glass door, and her throat clamped shut. She—a straight-A student and four-time class president, whose hand was always first in the air whenever a teacher asked a question—turned mute.

In the years that followed, she never knew when it would happen next. There were times she could deliver a wedding toast or make a presentation before a group of lobbyists, no problem. And then there were the times, just as frequent, that her voice shrank and vanished. In 2010, she was promoted in her job as staff liaison to a trade association in Washington, D.C. But she didn't celebrate; she panicked. Her boss wanted her to shine, and there was no mistaking what he meant: bigger presentations, more important conferences, wider exposure. Her house of cards was shaking. Always the good student, she cast around for help and found the Stagefright Survival School in Alexandria, Virginia, which promised help for "*extreme* fear of public speaking." Its cofounder, Burton Rubin, was, like Gutierrez, a lawyer who had built his career around the avoidance of public speaking.

Rubin's personal knowledge of stage fright began in grade school when, as the narrator of a school play, he became so immersed in the spectacle that he missed his cue and blew his lines. "I was having such a good time watching the play, I forgot I was supposed to be in it," he said. In his eight-year-old mind, he had ruined the whole production, and though his classmates forgot all about it, he never did. Rubin spent the rest of his school years with his head down, hiding at the back of the classroom, praying that he would not be called on. Mostly, he succeeded. When he graduated from the University of North Carolina School of Law in 1969, few of his professors recognized his face or knew his name. Over the next twenty years, he tried psychotherapy, cognitive behavior therapy, hypnosis, biofeedback, and group therapy—all to ease his terror of public speaking. Nothing worked as well as avoidance, which is why, instead of practicing law, he went into legal publishing, a field in which he assumed he would never have to speak in public again.

Over the years, Rubin spent so much time in group therapy that he became one of the group's leader. It was an intensive program for people with a variety of phobias, including fear of heights and enclosed spaces. The approach was based on the theory of contextual therapy: If a client was afraid of elevators, Rubin's job would be to ride up and down an elevator with him. If a person had a fear of bridges, Rubin would get in a car with him and drive across a mile-long span. But when it came to public speaking—*his* fear—there was nothing. In 1984, he found David Charney, a Washington-area psychiatrist with a specialty in anxiety disorders. With Charney's counseling, Rubin began to make headway. "It was a catalytic process of my being able to talk with him on a professional basis, with him being able to address it from the outside and me seeing it from the inside," he said. "It made me able to manage my symptoms so I could function." Charney taught him to quiet his internal fear-talk. "You can always engage in that thinking that will provoke the response. It's the self-conscious thought process. As soon as you become conscious of yourself, focus on yourself, you've put yourself in danger. We have to give people a way to prevent them from thinking about themselves."

A few years later, Rubin and Charney founded the Stagefright Survival School—Charney lecturing on and dealing with medical issues, including the prescribing of beta-blockers and Xanax; Rubin leading classes of mostly lawyers, diplomats, bureaucrats, entrepreneurs, physicians, and teachers. The meetings were sometimes reminiscent of a twelve-step program, and the overlap was perhaps more than coincidental. According to Rubin, "One tragedy in the early days was to see that before they reached us, some of our clients turned to alcohol as a way to self-medicate their performance anxiety."

Rubin is a genial, avuncular man with a propensity for thinking out loud and drawing emphatic conclusions. "Everybody
who has this anxiety tends to have an obsessive-compulsive,
perfectionist sort of personality," he declared. "As perfectionists,
they are intolerant of their own levels of anxiety. They desire at
all times to appear totally calm and collected, so their own background level of anxiety is unacceptable to them. Which raises
their anxiety even more." With his own anxiety under control,
Rubin opened a private law practice in 2004. Already in his
sixties, he wanted a taste of what it was like to actually practice
law. He litigated several consumer cases, an experience that both
fascinated and horrified him. "Judges, like law professors, can be
quite condescending and ridiculing," he said. "From a performance anxiety perspective, it's a huge challenge."

Gutierrez, for her part, attended Rubin's classes for six
months, always in secret. She never told her fiancé where she
went after leaving the office on Monday evenings. Nor did
she tell him after they were married. Every week, she stood in
front of the group like a recovering alcoholic ("I felt like I
should say, 'My name is Martha Gutierrez and I have public-
speaking anxiety' "), reading passages aloud from whatever
book Rubin thrust in her hands. She learned to slow down
and become more deliberate in her speech, a technique that
soothed and helped reverse some of the fast, feverish chatter
that took control whenever she found herself alone at the
podium. She incorporated Rubin's many tricks, including his
suggestion to use "prompting," jotting a word or phrase in the
corner of her notes as a way of distracting herself from the
self-conscious thoughts that took over whenever she had to

make a presentation. *Frog, table, phone*, she scribbled in the margins of her notes. To her amazement, it helped. She discovered that when she was in a panic, she had only to stare at the word, to *really* focus on it and imagine the grain of the wood in the tabletop or the feel of the frog's skin beneath her fingers. By focusing on something other than her fear, she found that she could stop running. But her Eureka! moment came when she watched a video of herself speaking before a group of her classmates. She wasn't all that bad.

These days, she makes presentations to audiences of about fifty, and she knows the time will come when she is expected to address hundreds. "I have improved so much, it's no longer an issue," she said. "I'm not a great speaker. It's something I'll always have to work on. But sometimes I am so proud of myself, I think I'm amazing! Other times, well . . . Speaking is not one of my fortes, but now I let it go."

Attempts to measure fear of public speaking in the general population have yielded far-flung results, with estimates ranging from 30 to 70 percent. A 2014 survey by the online research and consulting firm YouGov reported that 56 percent of Americans were "very" or "a little" afraid of public speaking. But it wasn't their top-ranking fear; snakes and heights ranked higher. Among the British, YouGov found the same prevalence of public-speaking anxiety, but that figure exceeded a fear of heights and snakes.

University textbooks for decades have propagated the notion that "people fear public speaking more than death." That understanding is based on a 1973 survey by R. H. Bruskin

Associates, a now defunct marketing company that identified public speaking as the most common of American fears. In 2010, two researchers in the School of Communications at the University of Nebraska at Omaha decided to follow up on that survey by asking 815 college students to select and then rank their fears from a list that included death, heights, darkness, financial problems, and deep water. According to their findings, 61.7 percent of students selected public speaking more often than any other fear. But when it came to ranking their fears, a slight majority (20 percent) identified death as number one, followed by public speaking at 18.4 percent.[1]

Early in his career, James McCroskey, a prolific scholar in the field of communication studies, found a direct correlation between public speaking and suicide. His interest was sparked after he received a phone call one evening in 1965 from a psychologist inquiring about one of McCroskey's students at Pennsylvania State University. The psychologist wanted to know if the student was scheduled to present a speech the following day. "I informed him that she did [sic]," McCroskey later recounted.[2] "I asked him why he wanted to know. He informed me that they had just rescued this student from an attempt to commit suicide by jumping off the top of one of the highest buildings at the university. She had indicated that she just could not face having to give another speech."

Alarmed, McCroskey began digging and, with a colleague, persuaded the university administration to release the names of the students who had committed suicide in recent years, along with enrollments in required speaking classes. "There were fourteen suicides recorded, and all but one of those students were currently enrolled in required public-speaking classes at the time of their death. Was this just coincidence? Possibly, but the odds are strongly against it."

At the time, many universities had a public-speaking requirement for graduation, but McCroskey's research convinced him that it should be dropped. In addition to the number of suicides, he was concerned over the issue of "reticent students," those whose fear levels couldn't be distinguished from those of their classmates. On further investigation, he concluded that "there may be hundreds or even thousands of students who drop the course, change their major to one that doesn't require a public-speaking class, or even transfer to another school that doesn't have that requirement." When a few years later, in 1972, he became chair of the Department of Communication Studies at West Virginia University, he ended the requirement and developed an interpersonal communication class that did not include public speaking. Within four years, enrollment in the department had tripled.

There are virtual reality programs that will take you into an office with a handful of people sitting around a conference table. You're there for an interview, but the people you've come to impress look bored. Don't freak out yet, though—wait until you get to the packed auditorium. Clinical psychologist Elizabeth Jane McMahon, who uses these programs in her San Jose practice, has had to talk numerous patients down as they sat behind a set of goggles, sweating, hyperventilating, becoming nauseated. The two-dimensional scenery and spectators look real enough to trigger their anxieties of public speaking.

With McMahon beside them, reminding them to breathe and asking them to rate their anxiety level, their fears often subside, she said, in as few as six or eight sessions. Virtual reality therapy is especially useful for patients who are too anxious to undergo real-life exposure. According to McMahon, public speaking is among the hardest fears to treat—harder than the fear of flying. The dangers of flying are at least definable: In 2012, there were 119 worldwide crashes and 794 deaths. You can read the numbers, put them in context, and plan your next step. But with public speaking, the dangers are subjective, internal, and mysterious: A pause, a stutter, the wrong word, and it's all over. In the mind of the speaker, he's crashed and burned. The reality of one's own performance is distorted as through a fun-house mirror; by comparison, everybody else looks airbrushed perfect.

"Most people get anxiety when they're facing their fear in virtual reality," McMahon says. "And generally, their fear drops relatively quickly if they do cognitive behavior therapy while they're in that virtual environment. It bridges that gap of talking about it and going out in reality and doing it totally on your own. So you go into 'reality' with a therapist there, guiding you, asking you, 'What are your worst fears?' Maybe they're afraid they're going to look stupid, or they're afraid the audience will hear their voice tremble. I make sure they have a technique to tolerate the anxiety—some slow belly breathing, while we're in the virtual reality."

For those willing to step out from behind the goggles and into the limelight, there is always Toastmasters, with its 14,650 chapters and 313,000 members in 126 countries. The meetings are free and open to the public, and if you are willing to listen to your fellow toastmasters' speeches about their trips in the RV, their grandchildren, and their cookie recipes, the rewards can be great. Every meeting begins with Table Topics, where a member directs questions about a topic of his choice to individuals in the audience who must stand and respond extemporaneously. Next come the prepared speeches, which are evaluated by everyone in the room. At the end of the meeting, a grammarian assesses the speakers' use of language and the numbers of "ums," "uhs," and "you knows" to which they resorted. Toastmasters is a low-cost education in public speaking. Its tips are basic yet invaluable. Among them: Know your material. Practice, rehearse aloud, and revise as needed. Use a timer. Know your audience, and greet them as they arrive. Get to know the room where you'll be speaking; arrive early and make yourself comfortable. Pause, smile, and count to three before saying a word. And don't apologize for being nervous; the audience probably hasn't even noticed.

Toastmasters has spawned many private workshops, each with its own spin. At the Self-Expression Center in Houston, Texas, psychologist Sandra Zimmer, a onetime actress, prods her clients to stand in front of the group and wait, silently, until "something shifts," as she puts it. Eventually, she promises, usually within a few minutes, their tension will begin to dissolve. They will relax into their bodies and learn to enjoy being the focus of attention. Because, according to Zimmer, stage fright is really just a fear of *feeling* in front of other people. She believes that the very act of standing up before a group is infantilizing. "The feelings that get stirred up when we are the center of attention make us vulnerable," she says. "The secret is to focus attention into your fear, into the sensations of tension in your body."

Her perspective bears resemblance to the Freudian view of performance anxiety as a reversion to infantile behavior, based on a dread of exposing oneself, of being naked and helpless in the eyes of the world. "The secret is to focus attention into your fear, into the sensations of tension in your body," Zimmer says. "Stage fright is passion energy that's stuck in the body and that's not being allowed to flow through. I once thought you had to thoroughly understand your issues to heal them, but now I believe healing is just a matter of having the freedom and permission to experience the emotions that got stuck in the body."

If it was easy, Tom Durkin might still be calling the Triple Crown. For thirteen years, he was the signature voice of the Kentucky Derby, the Preakness Stakes, and the Belmont Stakes, the three most coveted events in thoroughbred racing. He chucked it all in 2011, saying his mental health was more important than his career.

To be a horse-racing announcer was all he had wanted since his childhood days at the track in Chicago in the 1960s, first accompanied by his parents and later playing hooky with friends. But it wasn't the horses that piqued his interest so much as the announcer's booth, where Phil Georgeff, "the voice of Chicago racing" during the 1960s, sat and called the winners. Durkin stared up at his idol, wrote letters to him, asked for advice. Being at the track and hearing that voice— that was the height of excitement for Durkin, who related his story one afternoon while on his way to Belmont Park racetrack, where he still calls the winners.

At St. Norbert College in Wisconsin, he majored in theater because he thought it would help with his race announcing. Postgraduation in 1971, he called races from the back of a pickup truck on the county fair circuit, working his way up to modest tracks in the South and Midwest. By the time he was thirty-five, he was calling the Breeders' Cup Classic, one of the nation's premier races. He saw himself in every way ("genetically, emotionally, environmentally") as a performer.

But within a few years, he began to suffer anxiety attacks that brought waves of nausea whenever a big race neared. The potential for error lurked everywhere. Once, upon arriving at Churchill Downs in Louisville, Kentucky, for the Breeders'

Tom Durkin (Courtesy of New York Racing Association)

Cup, he discovered that a rainstorm had turned the track into a muddy course. He feared that when the race began, the horses would kick up enough mud to obscure the colors of the silks, the colorful jackets that distinguish one jockey from the other. Durkin had memorized the colors and now he was terrified that he would be unable to make the correct call. How was he to know which horse was which? With each new race came a new fear, reminding him of the dire warnings of the nuns from back in his Catholic school days: "Any mistake will be on your permanent record." The anxiety only magnified after he signed with NBC in 2001. It should have been a cakewalk: a weekend of work for a six-figure income. But instead of 120,000 people in the bleachers for the Preakness, he was now broadcasting live to an invisible audience of 20 million. "What's it like to be one easy mistake away from being a national joke?" a sports reporter asked him.

It was an offhanded comment, but it touched a nerve. The question suffused his nights, filling them with dreams so transparent that they hardly required an analyst's interpretation. In one, a cruise ship sailed down the final stretch of Churchill Downs, blocking his sight of the charging horses. The jockeys fell off their mounts and waged a tug-of-war, while a barbershop quartet sang and Durkin raged from the sidelines, "You can't do this! This is a horse race!" He tumbled out of his booth and landed on an awning eighty feet up in the air. "Watch out, mister!" a little boy shouted. "You're way off the ground."

Durkin tried medication, analysis, prayer, breathing exercises, hypnosis. He read widely on the subject and developed an affinity for Sir Laurence Olivier and his late-in-life stage

terrors. Before each racing season, Durkin trained like a mara-
thon runner, abstained from alcohol, and shed a good twenty
pounds. "Believe me, I was a monk," he told one reporter. He
had come close to quitting once, calling the president of NBC
Sports to give his resignation and then abruptly changing his
mind. This time, he stuck to his decision. He would continue
to call the smaller races at Belmont, Aqueduct, and Saratoga,
but at sixty-one, he was finished with the pressure of the big
races. Ending our conversation, he explained his change of
heart to me like this: "Let's say you're hitting your head with
a hammer. The first thing you do is mask the pain, so you take
an aspirin. It still hurts, so you put on a football helmet. But
it's still hurting. And it's hurting so much your brains are
rocking back and forth. At some point, you realize, 'What if I
didn't hit myself with a hammer?' "

The ancient Greeks had a word for this kind of sudden reversal
in self-understanding. They called it "anagnorisis," or recognition, the instant when a person discovers his or her mistaken-
ness. According to Aristotle, anagnorisis characterized the
highest form of drama. It is the moment that all great novels
turn on, the moment when the character realizes how
mistaken his or her sense of reality has been.[3] One thinks of
Pip in *Great Expectations*, his worldview shaken when he
discovers that his life's fortune was the behest of a miserable
convict. Or *Pride and Prejudice*, when Elizabeth Bennet realizes that everything she thought about Darcy was in error and
that his pride is not nearly as bad as her prejudice. Or, for that
matter, of Raskolnikov, the impoverished student of *Crime*

and Punishment, who murders an elderly pawnbroker and recognizes that his theory of the "great man," exempt from the laws that dictate human interaction, is wrongheaded.

In one way or another, these Eureka! moments figure in all our lives. They are the moments when we discover the falsehoods lurking in our most cherished beliefs. In life, as in literature, they are the catalyst for change. The change might be a decision just to walk away, as Durkin did, to the great relief of almost everyone who knew him. (All, that is, except his accountant.) Or they may signal a shift in one's own definition of success and failure, as happened to Martha Gutierrez when she watched the video recording of her speech at the Stagefright Survival School. She wasn't "that bad." McMahon, the psychologist, had a similar revelation a few years ago when she was being interviewed on TV for a segment about how to maintain one's mental health in bad financial times. She had never been on TV before, and as the cameras began rolling, the moderator casually mentioned that she hoped to get the footage in one take. "My heart was pounding, my throat was drawing in tight, and I wasn't sure I could even talk," McMahon recalled. "I said to myself, Get over yourself. This is not about you. This is an opportunity to give information that could be helpful to people who need it. Within seconds, my anxiety dropped."

Karolina Strassmayer never had a problem in performance as long as she was playing her saxophone. It was only when the music stopped and the audience waited for her to introduce the band, to announce the names of her tunes, and to make some welcome chitchat that she lost control. She wished she were like Dizzy Gillespie, the prankster who could charm and josh and set an audience at ease. Instead, she grew so nervous that she couldn't shut up. She talked and talked and could make no sense of anything she said. It was *that* bad. She saw the audience cringing in front of her; she sensed the band members flinching behind her. She was the only woman onstage, and suddenly she felt very far from home.

Strassmayer was born in Bad Mitterndorf, a postcard-perfect village in the Austrian Alps where her family has lived for generations. Her mother was a music teacher; her grandfather was the conductor of the town orchestra. It was assumed that Strassmayer, who grew up playing traditional Austrian music on the flute and recorder, would marry a local boy and take her place in the musical life of the town. But then something unforeseen happened. When she was sixteen, a friend's sister was throwing away some old unlabeled cassette tapes. Strassmayer rescued one and gave it a listen. It turned out to be trumpeter Miles Davis's *Kind of Blue*, and the sound of his band reached her ears like a fanfare from another world. She heard Cannonball Adderley blowing his heart out on the alto saxophone, and she knew she had to play what he was playing. Only none of her friends had ever heard an alto saxophone—certainly not the way he played it. She brought the tape to her grandfather, who guessed at the instrumentation, and within a few weeks Strassmayer had sold her mountain bike to buy a saxophone and take lessons with a teacher who had studied jazz in America.

Her new passion drove a subtle wedge between her and her friends and family. They thought the music was ugly. They said the saxophone wasn't a girl's instrument. At twenty-five, she moved to New York, armed with a scholarship to the New School, a visa, and little else. New York is where she came into her own, as a woman and as a musician. In time, she played in Carnegie Hall and at the Village Vanguard, often as not the only woman in the band. Her confident musicianship began drawing attention and she was soon featured in jazz magazines, where she inevitably was asked what it was like to be a woman in a world dominated by men. She always rebuffed the question with the same answer: She played just like anyone else.

But that came at a cost. At the New School, a teacher once told her that she would always "have to be better than the guys, or no one's going to take you seriously." She took the advice literally and played "like a man," blowing aggressively, especially on the first song of a set, just to prove the bandleader's faith in hiring her. It was an implicit response to the often explicit admonition that "I got a lot of flak for giving you the gig, so now you better deliver the goods." She played the horn with such force that she sustained stress-related injuries in her neck, shoulder, and back.

Strassmayer dressed "like a man," too, favoring leather jackets and trousers. She kept her hair short and eschewed makeup, "so no one could accuse me of dating the drummer or sleeping with the bandleader or looking cute onstage." She knew she was being scrutinized, and by now, she was scrutinizing herself. By the time she became a bandleader, her perfectionist qualities had reached new levels.

"I had so many expectations of myself, including being a Dizzy Gillespie kind of leader who made jokes and could be charming and wonderful, a perfect leader . . . I was twenty-seven or twenty-eight and I couldn't be all of those things. I'm not a natural entertainer. I was standing there petrified, talking myself into a tizzy and not getting a good reaction from the audience. They were cringing and so was I. Like, 'I can't believe I just said that.' And the looks from people in the audience: *Oh God, don't say anything, just play.*"

Some jazz musicians never say a word onstage; her hero, Miles Davis, rarely did. But the advice of her mentor at the New School hung in the air, reminding her that as the only woman onstage, she had to prove herself. Whenever one of the other musicians took a solo, she found herself obsessing over what she would say when the tune ended. Would the audience like her? How could she get them to laugh? How should she introduce the bass player? "Now in hindsight," she says, "I think that being a woman affected my performance anxiety."

Strassmayer spent years studying the Alexander technique, a system of movement that teaches coordination of gestures, muscle relaxation, and deep breathing. It focuses on physical alignment and poise. Musicians often turn to it when they are injured; it helps them unlearn maladaptive habits and deal with the stress of performance and repetitive motion. Though Strassmayer found it valuable, she benefited more from psycho-therapy, which helped her come to a détente with her fear. "It helped me become myself and be happy with that," she said. "The root of performance anxiety was always not being okay with myself—my skills, my looks, or whatever. Not living up to my own expectations, which were off the chart at that time."

In 2004, she was offered a place in the WDR Big Band in Cologne, Germany. The position brought instant credibility;

the WDR Big Band is one of the best jazz ensembles in Europe. Strassmayer no longer felt she had to prove herself on a daily basis. Though still the only woman onstage, she could relax and feel confident in her musicianship. She created her own band, KLARO! ("No Sweat" in German, a wordplay on her nickname, Karo), with her husband, jazz drummer Drori Mondlak, and their music began garnering enthusiastic reviews.

"I'm a product of a generation of women who saw that their mothers were very dissatisfied being stay-at-home moms. I remember promising myself very early on that I was not going to be that. I was going to go out in the world and do something. Not just be a hobby musician, but someone who makes the best of herself. That was a guiding principle. Today I can enjoy that drive."

Now, when a tune ends and it's time to introduce the band, Strassmayer can speak with ease and even joy. A present-moment awareness—feeling the breath, the body, the sound of the instrument, the temperature in the room, physical sensations—is the key. "When performance anxiety happens today, I don't engage in it. I can say, 'Oh, here it is.' It's sort of like a recognition of a thought or a pattern that wants to reinstate itself. But there's enough awareness not to buy into it. That gives me great freedom to enjoy myself onstage. I've also learned that it helps me to think of the audience not as an anonymous, potentially hostile crowd, but rather as individuals. And I speak to them as individuals, not with a hard focus on a single person, but [with] a soft focus that sweeps over individual faces, lingers for a moment on one face, and moves on."

Chapter 11

CULTURAL ARTIFACTS OF FEAR

"BENJAMIN" IS A forty-eight-year-old Orthodox Jew who lives in northern Jerusalem with his wife and eight children. He is a scholar who has spent his life immersed in Jewish studies and is admired by his community for his erudition and expertise in ancient manuscripts. But for as long as he can remember, Benjamin has had a fear of appearing and speaking in public. At wedding parties, he leaves before the final prayers, to avoid being asked to recite a blessing. He declines to read the haftarah (the weekly portion from the Books of the Prophets) in his synagogue, and though he is very religious, he stays home on Saturdays because he is afraid of being called to the Torah. He gets anxious before saying the blessing over wine on Friday nights with his family, and if a stranger is invited for the Sabbath dinner, his anxiety grows extreme.

This portrait of Benjamin, as drawn by the Israeli psychiatrist David Greenberg, is the only published account of an unusual social phobia known as *aymat zibur*.[1] The disorder takes its name from a Hebrew term that translates literally as "fear of the community." As described by Greenberg, director of the Community Mental Health Center at Herzog Hospital in Jerusalem, it is a form of performance anxiety that's specific to ultra-Orthodox Jewish men—and only men, since the women of this community are not permitted to lead prayers.

Aymat zibur is an expression that derives from a single passage in the Babylonian Talmud, which dates back to the sixth century. It refers to the sense of awe and respect demanded of a priest who serves as intermediary between God and man. In the words of the text: "Rabbi Isaac said: Let respect for the congregation be always upon thee; for behold, the *kohanim* [priests] had their faces toward the people and their backs toward the *Shechinah* [a Hebrew name for God]."

Scholars of Jewish law acknowledge the incongruity of this passage. One would expect a priest to show more respect for God's presence by facing It, rather than turning his back. The text suggests that the fear of the community is strong enough even to overcome the fear of God. Or perhaps the priest's responsibility to the community is so enormous, so onerous, that it merits a degree of fear. But in recent years, the meaning has shifted from a term of esteem to one of distress. When *aymat zibur* is mentioned in contemporary medical journals, it is cited as a culture-specific anxiety disorder, along the lines of the Cambodian *pul meunuh*, which literally means "poisoning by people"; the Japanese *taijin kyofusho*, which refers to a fear of interpersonal relations; or the Indian *dhat*, a folk term sometimes translated as "semen-worry." In all these cases, societal norms play a critical role in determining when behavior turns pathological. They are culture-specific variants of performance anxiety writ large.

Though Greenberg refrains from estimating the prevalence of *aymat zibur,* he quotes the rough calculations of a *gabbai* in a large Hasidic synagogue in Jerusalem. A *gabbai* is someone whose function resembles that of a churchwarden or sexton; he's the person who helps organize activities and services and selects people to recite the weekly benedictions. According to this *gabbai,* 30 percent of his synagogue's congregants decline to stand up and perform the prayers. "Those with difficulties seem to fear they will get stuck saying the prayers aloud or will stutter," he is quoted. Not very scientific, but a surprisingly high number all the same.

Greenberg draws his own seven examples from a caseload of five hundred ultra-Orthodox male referrals. One young man, identified as "Ezekiel," came self-diagnosed to the psychiatrist's clinic. "I was asked to be hazan [leader of prayers] on the Sabbath and practiced for a few weeks, but I have *aymat zibur* with a stutter, and did not want to shame myself in front of the Holy Ark, so my mother agreed it is unnecessary to shame myself," Ezekiel told the psychiatrist. "As a child, I knew the tunes, but the pressure and fear ruined it all. My brother also doesn't lead prayers—there are many with 'fear of the congregation.' "

Aymat zibur becomes a problem when it thwarts fulfillment of the very obligations that mark ultra-Orthodox Jewish men as members of their community. Fear of performance may prevent them from leading prayers (a religious duty expected of every adult male) and reciting the blessings over the Torah (which is considered an honor). "If, as a result of this problem, a sufferer does not attend public prayer, he is avoiding an integral part of religious life," Greenberg writes. "If a mourner does not lead the prayers during the year of mourning, this will be immediately noted. He has first right to the honor, and will feel uncomfortable at not doing so."

For the man called Benjamin, the distress is simultaneously chronic and anticipatory. When his daughters become pregnant, he worries well in advance of the birth that if a boy is born, he—the grandfather—will have to assume a role in the bris, or ceremonial circumcision. He frets about the eventuality of his parents' deaths ("May they live many years"), anticipating that he will have to lead the congregation in the daily Kaddish, or prayer of mourning, in the year that follows a loved one's demise. His blushing signals the onset of a domino effect: His voice chokes, his legs tremble, he becomes convinced that everybody within eyesight sees and stares at him, which makes him blush all the more.

Many men who suffer from *aymat zibur* appear to have been shy or anxious children. Their anxieties were overlooked, probably because a timid and taciturn personality blends smoothly into a culture that shuns secular society and values above all else the keeping of Jewish law. Teenage boys commonly study Torah to the near exclusion of all other activities. The ancient teachings are filled with exhortations discouraging social intercourse and easy conversation. "Whoever stops studying Torah in order to engage in conversation is fed the embers of a broom fire," a passage in the Talmud warns. In the ultra-Orthodox world, a man's worth is measured by the study of Torah, and any conversation that takes away from that study is discouraged. Greenberg quotes Maimonides thus: "A person should excel in silence and should not speak, unless to say matters of wisdom or matters to do with physical needs."

But while a natural reserve may be admired and even encouraged, a man's ultimate standing in the community rests largely on his voice. The *talmid haham*, or wise student, is sought after for public speaking (on religious subjects, naturally) at social gatherings and ceremonies. And in the world of the ultra-Orthodox, teaching Torah confers the highest status of all; it's the equivalent of being a cardiologist in the secular Jewish world. Effectively barred from so many activities integral to religious life, some of the younger men in the Jerusalem synagogue have tried group therapy to improve their public-speaking skills. In some cases, according to Greenberg, they have turned to a *shidduch*, or matchmaker, perhaps hoping that a wife would help ease their way into society. Benjamin turned to his rabbi. When that proved unhelpful, he sounded out Kabbalists—mystical sages—for counseling, blessings, and remedies. "Sorcerers," he told the psychiatrist dismissively. "If not for this problem, I would have opened a school."

The term *aymat zibur* is barely known outside ultra-Orthodox Judaism, but its effects permeate well beyond those confines. Corinne Blackmer is a member of Beth El-Keser Israel Congregation, a Conservative synagogue in New Haven, Connecticut. BEKI, as it is known, is an egalitarian congregation where women are allowed and encouraged to read from the Torah. Blackmer regards it as her second home and regularly attends Saturday services. But put her on the bimah, the podium from which the Torah is read, and she exhibits many of the same symptoms as the ultra-Orthodox Israeli men who suffer from *aymat zibur*. The last time she stood for the honor she opened her mouth, blurted out a few words, and fled the synagogue. The Hebrew language isn't her problem. Blackmer speaks it fluently. She lived in Israel for several years and fought with the Israel Defense Forces during the Yom Kippur War of 1973. Nor is she afraid of public speaking. A professor of English and Judaic Studies at Southern Connecticut State University, she routinely lectures before hundreds, loves to speak before large groups, and earns excellent ratings from her students.

Her anxiety is specific to liturgical Hebrew. Though she knows the prayers by heart, she is afraid to get up and chant them. "I feel intimidated by the congregation since there are so many accomplished people there. Even though they are incredibly nice." In a sense, chanting Torah is not all that different from performing a classical music recital, with its zero tolerance for error. The instant a reader mispronounces a word in the Torah, or even stresses the wrong syllable, the members of the congregation are duty-bound to correct her—literally stopping the performance and forcing her to acknowledge and redress her mistake. For Blackmer, the delicacy of the parchment scroll itself creates an added anxiety. "I don't want to hurt it," she says. "I'm afraid that I might take the Torah pointer and jab it through. I've literally thought of that." Though she can easily read the daily prayers, she is studying them intensely, hoping to one day stand up and recite them comfortably.

The most examined of culture-specific anxieties is the Japanese *taijin kyofusho*, which translates as a fear of interpersonal relations. *Taijin* is almost the flip side of performance anxiety as we know it in the West. Instead of fearing that you are going to embarrass yourself with your behavior, you fear that you will embarrass or even offend others by your very presence. In the Japanese diagnostic system, there are four subtypes of the disorder: *sekimen-kyofu* (the fear of blushing), *shubo-kyofu* (the fear of a deformed body), *jikoshisen-kyofu* (the fear of eye-to-eye contact), and *jikoshu-kyofu* (the fear of one's own foul body odor). Most sufferers experience only one of these fears.

Taijin kyofusho is especially prevalent among adolescent boys and young men; studies report that 10 to 20 percent of Japanese males say they suffer from it. When a Japanese psychophysiologist, who examines the impact of fear and other emotions on the body, confided to me that she had *taijin*, I wondered if she was joking. It turned out that she had studied to be a concert pianist until perfectionism got in the way. "If there is a very small mistake, it ruins my performance," she said, explaining that a serious case of focal dystonia—pianist's cramp—forced her to quit the piano entirely. The physical problem was exacerbated by her *taijin kyofusho*. "I worried that if I played bad music, people would be embarrassed." Now here she was, studying those very symptoms in other people, in her role as psychophysiologist.

The disorder was first described in 1919 by Japanese psychiatrist Shoma Morita, who classified it as part of a nervous temperament called *shinkeishitsu*, a condition that involves a high degree of perfectionism. Morita regarded it as a distinctly Asian disorder, and psychiatry has generally endorsed that view. According to a paper[2] in the 2010 *Journal of Depression and Anxiety*, "Social fears are very much dependent on a particular culture." In other words, a culture is expressed through its specific disorders just as surely as it is expressed through its art and music. "We are an individualistic culture, in which the individual is at the center of everything," said Stefan Hofmann, a Boston University psychologist and one of the authors of that study. "Japan is a collectivist society, and it's been shown in studies that these relationship fears, the fear of offending others, are unique to Japan, where close attention is typically paid to other people's thoughts and feelings."

Morita prescribed a treatment plan that combined a traditional form of Japanese psychotherapy with mindfulness meditation practices, physical activity, and self-acceptance techniques. The eponymous Morita therapy began with a period of isolated bed rest, during which patients were forbidden to read, listen to the radio or television, or indulge in conversation. In the second stage, they remained isolated but could leave their beds and engage in light work and simple chores. Under a therapist's guidance, they wrote in journals and read classical poetry out loud. Slowly and gradually, their freedoms were returned to them until eventually, usually by the sixth week, they attended lectures and meetings on self-acceptance. The original treatment plan lasted forty days, which sounds practically biblical. But when strictly followed, it was reported to have a success rate of 93.3 percent.

In India and Nepal, *dhat*, or semen-worry, is a folk term that describes a form of clinical depression in young men who suffer from premature ejaculation and impotence. The syndrome is bound up in a traditional Hindu belief system that deems semen the elixir of life, a fluid that is vital in the physical and mystical sense of the word. Young men with *dhat* seek medical help when they become convinced that they are passing semen in their urine, often during wet dreams. In some cases, they report that their penises have diminished in size. Their fear translates as a loss of male power. Doctors say there is no physical explanation; the cause is obsessive rumination.

While the acculturation of medical conditions has sometimes been dismissed as a relic of European imperialism, the most current (fifth) edition of the *DSM* lists nine culture-bound disorders. One of them is the Cambodian *khyal cap*, a form of panic attack that typically ends in a dead faint. *Khyal* is said to be a windlike substance that rushes through the body, fills the lungs, impedes breathing, and enters the heart, causing palpitations. It surges through the brain, shoots from the eyes, and floods the ear canals.

A *khyal* attack is often triggered by *pul meunuh*, or "poisoning by people." It can happen in any crowded space, but, like *aymat zibur*, it frequently occurs in a religious setting—in this case, a Buddhist temple, usually on festival days, when the devotee has to present an offering to the monk. Suddenly, he is in the limelight. All eyes in the temple are upon him as he kowtows, or bows, three times, presents his offering, and then raises his hands to receive a blessing from the monk.

"When they're in large groups, they will often say, and be very articulate about it, that when they look from face to face, they smell the different people," says Devon Hinton, a medical anthropologist and psychiatrist at Harvard Medical School, who has written extensively on *pul meunuh*. A majority of his patients, who come from the Cambodian immigrant community in the Boston suburbs, complain of the disorder. "They will want to orient to the different smells that are present. They are over-whelmed by stimuli, as they put it. It induces dizziness, a very dramatic version of it. It can be debilitating. They can't go to the temple, because they are afraid they can die from this."

Pul meunuh often manifests as a form of post-traumatic stress disorder, dating to the Cambodian civil war and geno-cide. Under the Khmer Rouge, whose regime lasted from 1975 to 1979, a quarter of the population died by starvation, forced labor, and execution. But even these experiences are only a catalyst. In fact, the history of *pul meunuh* extends back through many generations. "Even before Pol Pot, they would explain it as poisoning by people—the idea that you're up there and suddenly you smell other people," says Hinton. "It's how they explain not being able to perform."

Given the religious and existential overtones of such disorders, it should come as no surprise to find performance anxiety in pastors, preachers, and other religious leaders. Few publicly mention it or even acknowledge that their weekly sermons are performances of sorts. A number of divinity schools rebuffed my inquiries about programs to help young ministers get over their shakes. "We don't have that problem," one prominent Baptist dean informed me. Maybe not, but the physical mani-festations of performance anxiety are exactly what one Kansas parishioner found so endearing about her new minister. She wrote about it on her blog: "Yes, our pastor suffers from stage fright. His hands shake and his mouth gets dry and sometimes he loses his voice and has to pause. Which might sound like a bad thing, but it's something I love about him. He could never be a pastor on his own power. But the fact that he gets up in front of the congregation every Sunday and teaches us something new is a testament to the power of God."

The pastor's name was Larry Smith, and when I tracked him down in Topeka and read him what his parishioner had written, he sounded taken aback. There was a long silence on the other end of the phone line. "Yes," he finally said, "that sounds like me." I flew to Topeka, where I shared my own issues with performance anxiety and learned that Smith had an even longer and more complicated story to tell—one that began with easy money, alcohol, and profligacy and culminated in born-again Christianity.

As a young man in the 1970s and early 1980s, he had it all: a construction job that paid a munificent $32.50 an hour, "plus $50 a day just to show up." He and his wife, Laura, owned forty-five acres in Northern California, along with boats, cars, trucks, and tractors. But he was an alcoholic who daily washed down a fifth of gin with a twelve-pack of beer. He was also an obsessive gambler, "a very unhappy person." Then, at age thirty-six, "the Lord took it all away," the good and the bad. Smith was struck with a rare condition called thoracic outlet syndrome that numbed the nerves in his hands and arms. Complications set in, and his back swelled to twice its normal size. His neck muscles grew so large that whenever he laughed he passed out, he said. Smith was close to death when the doctors told his wife to get his affairs in order. Sitting beside him in his hospital room, she told him that he had to "find the Lord." And that's when, with his wife's help, he got down on his knees to ask forgiveness for his sins, was born again, and "wound up with this public-speaking problem." In that order.

No longer strong enough to work in construction, Smith enrolled at Sierra Community College near Sacramento, California. The classwork came easily to him. He had always been a good, if lazy, student. But in his second year, he took a public-speaking class, a requirement for transferring to a four-year university, and the first time he stood up to talk, he began to cry. "It almost shattered me. All the ugliness revealed itself in all its ugly ways. Shaking head, knees shaking, voice cracking. Most of the students were seventeen- to twenty-one-year-olds. They didn't know how to respond at first, they made fun of me."

They stopped laughing when the teacher, Mrs. Battenberg—Smith remembered her name with affection—stepped in. She arranged for him to tutor his classmates in algebra, his best subject, and encouraged him to keep talking. He printed his speeches out in large block letters to help him stay on track when the rush of noradrenaline so blurred his vision that he could barely read the words on the page. Nor did the problem improve when he transferred to Oregon State University in 1989. As public affairs director of student affairs, he was occasionally asked to give a speech—an effort that made him violently ill, to the point that he sometimes frightened the audience. One time, while delivering a talk at halftime during a football game, he said, "I thought I was going to die." His classmates pressed tight against him to keep him standing.

The fear of speaking didn't stop his choice of career. "God may have placed it there so I would remain humble and do all things for Him instead of on my own," Smith said. He was working on his master's degree at Western Seminary in Portland when he was unexpectedly solicited by Ariel Ministries, an evangelical group whose sole mission is the conversion of Jews. Would he be willing to go to Russia and convert the Jews of St. Petersburg?

Now it was my turn to be surprised. I toyed with the idea of saying something. Should I casually mention that my mother's grandparents were Russian Jews from St. Petersburg? That they had permits to reside in St. Petersburg, then Petrograd, at a time when Jews were largely proscribed from life in the city—unless they happened to be university students, intellectuals, wealthy businessmen, or skilled craftsmen? According to family legend, my great-grandfather was a cabinetmaker who had built the interior of the czar's train. I thought of the intricate, hand-carved rocking chair he made for my grandmother's wedding day. It was sitting in my living room back home, the only thing left of that generation in my family. "For fifteen years, we were the only outreach to the Jewish community," Smith continued, rocking me out of my reverie. "It was a very successful outreach—the only messianic missionary service in all of St. Petersburg. Hundreds of people came, people who didn't know anything about Judaism except that they were Jewish. We were a long time in Russia."

"A long time in Russia," repeated Laura. She had a habit of repeating the last few words of every sentence her husband spoke.

As it happened, the Russians had little sympathy for Smith's stage fright. Unlike the Kansas blogger, they did not find it charming. On the contrary, they were horrified. Smith, who lived in Russia nearly fifteen years, understood. "I was the pastor and the professor, the one with the knowledge and the power. People there expected a certain level of competence and decorum from someone with that status. When I broke down, they didn't like it. Some of them were angry. Some of them were disappointed in me. They would come up afterwards and say, 'Pastor, you can't do that.' My response was, 'I'll probably do it again, pray for me.' Some of them left and didn't come back. But the ones who got to know me got used to it."

Now Smith is back in Kansas, and after twenty years of preaching his voice still cracks, his hands clutch the lectern, his knees quake. Some of his American parishioners, like many of his congregants in St. Petersburg, ask why, if he is truly called by God, he is so nervous. Maybe if he had more faith, they suggest, God would heal him. The weekend I flew to Topeka to watch him preach, his head started aching on Friday. By Saturday night, he was in the bathroom with an upset stomach. "Yes," he said, "it's what the Lord has me doing." It was a part of his life, and he had developed strategies to make it through Sunday services. He always looked for his wife in the audience. He printed out his sermons in a large font, just as Mrs. Battenberg once taught him. He never stopped moving or drinking water.

The Sunday of my visit, he gripped the lectern and rocked back and forth. At sixty-three, he looked, with his white handlebar mustache, like the Wizard of Oz. It was a hot day in August, and the ceiling fans whirred overhead. The buzz competed with the sound of a tractor engine in a nearby corn-field, where a farmer was plowing under the year's crop. Everywhere one drove in Kansas that drought-filled summer, the fields were the color of straw. Smith's sermon focused on what I had come to recognize as his great passion, the all-important business of conversion.

He spoke with an almost painful hesitation. "Say you're out in the middle of Timbuktu, Kansas. I know we don't have a Timbuktu, but you're out in the middle of nowhere and you're witnessing to a farmer who wants to be baptized. What's to stop you?"

"Nothing," Laura called out from a pew in the middle of the church. About thirty people were scattered through the newly painted sanctuary.

"Who does the baptism?"

"You do," she called.

"That's right." He nodded. "There's absolutely nothing . . . nowhere in the Bible does it say you have to be a church leader." He paused noticeably, rocking from one foot to the other. "You find a water spout and let them make a profession of faith and they're following Jesus."

His hands shook as he soldiered on. "You know, you know," he started to say. "You know . . ." He appeared to have lost his train of thought. "I'm nervous. I'm excited. I might get a little emotional, so bear with me." He stopped to drink some water. "Each one of us who has professed faith has received a gift, and we are to use it for the building up and serving of one another, so that others know Jesus Christ." His hands were shaking now. "Please turn to Ephesians [the tenth book of the New Testament]. A great book, I highly recommend it. It's a great book."

The sermon lasted half an hour—in truth, it felt somewhat longer—and the service ended soon after. When I stood up to say good-bye, Laura beamed and gave me a big hug. "I'm going to pray for you and your piano playing," she promised.

Chapter 12

GAME PLANS

AFTER A STORYBOOK YEAR as National League All-Star second baseman for the Los Angeles Dodgers, Steve Sax lost the ability to throw a ball. It began with an error during a game against the Montreal Expos in April 1983, early in his second season. The batter doubled to right center, sending the runner on first to third. The outfielder threw the ball to Sax, who should have held on to it; there was no pressure to throw. Instead, he hummed it wildly to home, where it skipped off the catcher's shin guard and skittered to the backstop. The man on third scored.

It was a dumb error and not terribly important, except that the next day he made another error. Then came another. If he kept on at this rate, he figured, he'd log 132 errors by season's end. He was twenty-three years old and had just been named Rookie of the Year. Now, for the first time in his life, he questioned himself. "And when fear and doubt set into your psyche, it will absolutely rob and suck out every chance of success that you have. That's what it did to me," he said, sitting behind the desk of his home office in Roseville, California, a well-to-do suburb of Sacramento. "It took over my confidence in doing the most rudimentary things. Like throwing the ball fifty feet to first base. I couldn't do it anymore."

The walls were hung with his team jerseys, all framed and glassed like prized artwork. The dining room table was stacked with brochures and handouts. Sax makes his living as a motivational speaker, and he was preparing for the influx of financial executives who would attend his next seminar. Inevitably, he would tell them about his baseball meltdown. Thirty years after the fact, it still defined him.

In the summer of 1983, Sax would make thirty errors, twenty-four of them in a three-month summer span as his collapse played out before a fascinated public. You didn't have to be a baseball fan to know about Steve Sax's fall from grace. The entire country knew. As a sportswriter for the *Houston Chronicle* wrote, "He would throw the ball into the dugout. He would throw it into the ground. Sometimes, he would hold the ball for what seemed an eternity, seemingly afraid of what would happen if he attempted another toss." ESPN led each night's broadcast with footage of his latest humiliation. Fans donned batting helmets, baiting Sax to throw at them in the stands. Letters poured in to the Dodgers' home office, offering advice ("Try to make an error. Then you won't"), derision ("You're a freak. I'm a girl and I can throw the ball better than you"), and death threats ("One more time and we're going to come and put a bullet in your head"). The nation's gamblers were incensed; Sax had made it impossible to place a bet on a Dodgers game. The letters got so bad that he finally had to turn them over to the FBI.

Some of his teammates avoided throwing Sax the ball, but Dodgers manager Tommy Lasorda refused to bench him. Many times, Lasorda would take him out onto the field before a game, blindfold him, and make him practice his toss. "And I'd throw it every single time right there, blindfolded, to the person at first. I hit him in the chest every single time. And then the game would start and I'd throw that sucker up to Section J somewhere. Here we'd go again, the whole wave of problems, starting over again. I wanted to give up."

On the road, after a game against the Phillies, the Dodgers went out for dinner at a restaurant owned by one of Lasorda's brothers in a Philadelphia suburb. Sax returned to his hotel room at three in the morning, too tired to take off his clothes or climb under the sheets. Hours later, as the sun began shining through the blinds, he reached for the covers and felt something on the pillow. He opened his eyes and made out a silhouette. The shape of an ear. Reaching out, he touched something greasy. He switched on the light and found himself staring into the bulging eyes of a dead pig.

"I flew downstairs and went to the concierge's desk and yelled out, 'There's a pig in my bed!' So we went up there and there was a note attached to the ear and it said, 'Sax, you better start playing better or else! Signed, the Godfather.' And the concierge flipped it over, and there was a parking ticket from Norristown. Tommy Lasorda had done this to me as shock therapy. And no, it didn't help."

When help did come, it arrived unexpectedly, from his ironfisted father, whom Sax had grown up respecting and fearing in equal measure. John Sax was a farmer and regional truck driver, "a very tough dude," a German immigrant who showed his gentle side to only one person—his wife, Nancy. The two had met as children, and Sax recalled how his father "doted on her and treated her like she walked on water." When Sax was six, the family moved to a farm just outside Sacramento, not far from the stuccoed McMansion where he now lives. He and his younger brother, Dave, helped run the farm whenever their father was on the road. The boys milked the cows, fed the chickens, and irrigated the fields. In their spare time, they played ball: pitching, hitting fungoes, and chasing baseballs through the fields. They ended up as teammates on the Dodgers. Today, they live across the street from each other in Roseville.

By the time Sax was in sixth grade, he was buying his own clothes. By his senior year of high school, he had moved out of the house to escape his father's anger—and his fist. He had once watched John Sax beat up a man at a traffic light. The Saxes were squeezed inside the family car—a Metropolitan coupe, one of the first American compacts ("And how he got himself and five kids in this car, I'll never understand, whether with WD-40 and a shoe bar")—when a young driver cut them off, flashing his middle finger. The light turned red before he could take off. "And my dad got out and went over and introduced himself to this guy," Sax recalled. "He was from the Vietnam War, he had his fatigues on, and he was biting my dad's finger. My dad reached in, pulled him out of the car, and hit him. Brrrrr. It was a combination punch. He actually broke the guy's nose. His head slid against the corner of the door and the windshield, and he took thirty-two stitches in his ear." Sax knows this because the local sheriff was his uncle. "It was a bloody mess. My dad got back in the car and had to wait for the light to turn green. That's how fast it happened."

But John Sax also was a man of stubborn pride and fortitude. Once, while suffering a slipped disk so painful that he couldn't lift his leg for weeks, he crawled past his son, through the house, and into the bathroom, where he ran himself a hot bath. "He never once looked up to say 'Hey, I need a hand' or 'I'm in pain' or 'Why me?' He just didn't want to put anybody out."

In 1983, when Sax was in the midst of the "yips"—what the rest of the world would from then on refer to as "Steve Sax syndrome"—he called home and confessed that he didn't know what to do. All his life, he had believed that if he worked hard enough, the rewards would be his. Now, he told his father, he went to bed with his fear. He woke up with it. He felt it sitting at the breakfast table. "Hey, one of these days," his father told him, "you're going to wake up and this throwing problem is going to be gone. I know because the same thing happened to me."

John Sax had played baseball in high school. He was, according to his son, a "darn good ballplayer," having beat out future major leaguer Woodie Held for shortstop—the position Held would later play for the New York Yankees and six other clubs. In Steve Sax's mind, his dad was the most powerful man alive. "I thought, Wow, my invincible, stronger-than-life dad! If he could go through it and it didn't affect him, then I'm not so bad. He said, 'It's not you. There's nothing wrong with you. It's just your confidence. You have to get it back one bit at a time. It's just like chopping down a tree. One chop at a time.' And that's the last time I spoke with him. Six hours later he died. Heart attack number five."

Sax, born in 1960, is a handsome man with a classic, chiseled face and silver hair. He's a health fitness fanatic and a black belt in karate, with an intense energy that's been channeled into years of positive thinking. And the motivational speaker is never far away when he talks about the great fight of his life. If anything, it sounds like a religious conversion. "So I said, Okay, I admit I have a problem. I'm going to challenge it, I'm going to dare it, and I'm going to bite it in the face and say, 'Let's get it on.' It was just not going to beat me. This became more than me playing baseball. It became much more than me being an athlete or worrying what it was going to do to my contract in the years that followed. It was about my salvation as a human being. What it came down to was, I had to adopt a purpose. I had to plant a flag and adopt a purpose. And the purpose was to beat it. The most important thing in my life at that time was to beat it. It was more important than my family, it was more important than baseball, it was more important than me. It was so important for me to beat it that I would have come within an inch of selling my soul to the devil to beat it. So I beat it."

Taking his father's advice, he attacked his fear as if it were a tree. Chop, chop, chop. When he fielded ground balls during batting practice, he pretended to be in the middle of a game. If he made an accurate throw to first, he slathered himself with praise and affirmation: "That was easy. Of course I can

Steve Sax (Courtesy of the Los Angeles Dodgers)

do that." The instant bat met ball and a grounder headed in his direction, he began counting the seconds in his head, making sure that his throw landed in the first baseman's glove in four seconds flat: "Because that's as fast as a runner can get to first base." Pregame practice became his performance, "so that I was able to relax and feed off the momentum I had at practice. I was more at ease when the real game began, because, in my mind, I had just been through a game."

He felt his confidence returning. "Everything you do in sports, whether it's fielding or hitting, it's a feeling you get. The rhythm and relaxation come together, and when you start feeling that, your confidence starts to grow." By the end of the 1983 season, Sax had logged thirty-eight consecutive error-free games. He was, to all appearances, "cured." His performance block had lasted only three months, but it would become the defining experience of his life. He would become a five-time All-Star. He would help the Dodgers win the 1988 World Series. He would set the New York Yankees record for most singles (171) in a season. But that three-month mystery is what most people still remember when they hear his name.

"You know how many go through this and don't beat it?" Sax slapped his right fist in an imaginary left glove. "Ask Chuck Knoblauch. Ask Bob Moose. Ask Steve Blass." He is listing some of baseball's most famous head cases. "Ask Davy Murphy. He had to be sent to the outfield. He lost his position as a catcher. Lots of people. Mackey Sasser lost his career." Sasser, a catcher for the Mets from 1987 to 1995, developed a paralyzing fear of tossing the ball back to the pitcher. He would pump it over and over again, unable to let go, as the fans gleefully counted the number of pumps and opposing players ran around the bases. "And this happened in my second year! I went on to play eleven years after that." Again, Sax smacked his fist. "Not only did I beat it, but when I went to New York—check the numbers, please!—I was the top-fielding second baseman in the American League in my position. Look at the numbers. You can look them up right now if you want."

Not for him the therapy, the hypnosis, the biofeedback, or any of the treatments that other wigged-out ballplayers have turned to in desperation. Sax did it on his own. For years, that's how he understood his comeback. It wasn't until 1995, standing in his mother's kitchen, that he appreciated the meaning of his father's pep talk. He was recounting that last conversation—"the same thing happened to me"—when she stopped him. "Your father and I were together since fifth grade," his mother said, "and he never had a throwing problem."

Sax leaned back from his desk to let the force of that information sink in. "He never had a throwing problem!" Sax repeated the words like the refrain of a hymn. "He just did that to help me get through this." The awe in his voice was genuine, though he'd probably told the story five hundred times. "For someone who never said 'I love you,' maybe he just did. The gift he gave me on the day he died, I could never replace that."

While endemic in sports, the yips are most common in baseball and golf, games that provide or perhaps punish players with long periods of time to ponder and perseverate. Psychologists call it "paralysis by analysis." In golf, the yips are characterized by a sudden jerk or tremor of the hand, usually while putting. Golfers are so fearful of the yips that many refuse to speak the word out loud. When the yips happen, they can be painfully memorable. Ben Hogan, one of the game's first superstars, developed a case late in his career. He would stand over a putt for what seemed like an eternity, unable to draw the putter back and begin his stroke. He eventually gave up the game because of it.

Fast-moving sports such as basketball, football, and tennis also have their head cases, but the breakdowns typically occur when the action slows. Basketball players choke at the free-throw line. In football, it's the placekickers who usually blow it. Tennis players freeze at the serve. One of the most memorable chokes in tennis history took place at the 2004 French Open, when Guillermo Coria faced off against fellow Argentinian Gastón Gaudio. Coria was the hands-down favorite. Known as El Mago, the Magician, for his lethal drop shots and unreturnable backhand, he moved like a gazelle. Across the net, Gaudio was the journeyman and knew it. He was reported to laugh at how out of his league he found himself. But it was Coria who froze. It happened at the serve. His body tightened. He sat down, nervously jiggling his left foot and claiming a physical cramp. The commentators called it a mental cramp. Coria kept double faulting, giving away the third and fourth matches, before flushing the fifth down the toilet. "I just thought too much," he later explained.

Overthinking is almost always the problem. "When people are concerned about themselves and their performance, they tend to try to control their movements in order to ensure an optimal outcome," writes psychologist Sian Beilock in *Choke: What the Secrets of the Brain Reveal About Getting It Right When You Have To*. "What results is that fluid performances— performances that run best largely outside of conscious awareness—are messed up."[1] To illustrate, she studied highly skilled college soccer players at her Human Performance Lab at the University of Chicago. When the players were instructed to pay close attention to their footwork, their dribbling grew clumsy and error-prone, as compared with the times they dribbled without instruction. Inversely, skilled golfers who were instructed to putt as quickly as possible showed consistent improvement.

Overthinking occurs when the left hemisphere—the side responsible for language and analytical thinking—outbalances the right, which is given to imagination, coordination, and visual acumen. Researchers have found that golfers who putt poorly under pressure exhibit heightened activity in the left hemispheres of their brains and diminished activity in the right hemispheres. The more your left hemisphere lights up, the more your right switches off. With this in mind, researchers at the Institute of Sports Psychology at the Technical University of Munich came up with an easy way to balance the brain: Clench your left fist. Since each hand is connected to the opposite side of the brain, clenching the left hand activates the right hemisphere. The researchers tested their theory on semiprofessional football players, tae kwon do black belts, and expert badminton players. It worked. The participants kicked, punched, sparred, and served—first in seclusion, then while being filmed or watched by a crowd of spectators. What the researchers discovered was that the players who clenched their fist or squeezed a soft ball with the right hand were significantly more likely to choke under pressure. Those who used their left hand performed the same as before or better. It helped them shift the balance of brain activity away from the

left side, allowing them to stop overthinking and let muscle
memory take over.

It was six weeks before my concert and I kept hearing about
the connection—and disconnect—between music and sports.
One pianist marveled over the way soccer coaches rushed
out on the field with an ice pack and bandage whenever
a player took a hard fall. As a conservatory student, she hesit-
ated to even mention to her teacher that she had injured her
hand from overpractice. A violinist wondered at how easily
Olympic athletes discussed their stress levels before a competition; none of the string players he knew admitted to having
nerves at an audition. Maybe, another violinist suggested,
musicians should take a lesson from pro golfers, who know
how to conjure an image of the perfect shot, cuing the image
with an emotion before they begin their swing.

I called Noa Kageyama, my performance coach at Juilliard,
remembering that he had been mentored by a sport psychologist named Don Greene. It was Greene who originally inspired
Kageyama to quit the violin and become a psychologist.

Kageyama put me in touch with Greene, who in his role as
adviser bounced between the highest echelons of sports and
music. In addition to his work with the U.S. Olympic Diving
Team, he consulted with professional golfers, tennis players,
and Grand Prix drivers. His specialty was training these
athletes to perform under pressure, but he had also established
a reputation for doing the same with musicians. He first took
an interest in their problems after a chance encounter with the
principal bassist of the Syracuse Symphony Orchestra (now

defunct). They met on a golf course in 1992, and when Edward Castilano learned what Greene did for a living, he asked the psychologist for help in improving his game. Greene ran him through a two-part inventory that he'd designed with the late Bruce Ogilvie, who is often referred to as "the father of sport psychology." Ogilvie was a professor of psychology at San Jose State University. He had been trained as a Freudian at the University of London's Institute of Psychiatry, and though he rejected some of Freud's teachings, he still spoke the language. He came to sports from a background of treating sexual inhibition as a performance anxiety problem. Once, after the Los Angeles Lakers approached the NBA Championship for the second year in a row, he observed, "Winning it all is like one great orgasm. A number of players must go through a quiescent state before they can reach 'psychological erection' again."

Ogilvie was of the mind that sexual dysfunction was the result of a disconnect between mind and body, and he applied that same theory to sports performance—to the mind-body disconnect in athletes. Combining techniques of visualization, relaxation, and role-playing, he developed performance enhancement strategies that would become the foundation of every sport psychologist's playbook.

Greene collaborated with Ogilvie on a sports inventory that codified these strategies. The first part, the Learning Styles Inventory, analyzed an athlete's psychological strengths and weaknesses in order to establish a baseline of treatment. The second part, called the Competitive Styles Inventory, examined how the same athletes performed under pressure. In drawing up these inventories, the two psychologists conducted three studies, each based on interviews with more than a thousand athletes. Greene half joked that the project cost him his marriage and plunged him into debt. In 1995, with nowhere else to go, he retreated to Ogilvie's estate, a thirty-seven-acre property in the Santa Cruz Mountains. The Cats Estate, as it is known, boasts some of the most prized views in Northern California. In its prime, it was visited by Charlie Chaplin, John Steinbeck, and Eleanor Roosevelt. Greene and Ogilvie dedicated two years at Cats to refining their sports inventories, but they never saw a payoff.

It was only years later, when Castilano asked for help with his golf putt, that Greene put him through the paces of the ninety-six-question inventory. It revealed that Castilano was motivated but tended to overthink his putts. Greene taught him how to center himself, quieting his thoughts, and the musician's putting quickly improved. Castilano recognized the potential benefit to musicians and coaxed Greene to Syracuse to work with the members of his orchestra. So began a whole new career for Greene and a whole new application of sport psychology. Initially, he assumed that music was "a totally different ball game," he told me. He was a jock who didn't know and didn't care about classical music.

But performance anxiety was something he knew firsthand. In high school in the late 1960s, he had been a competitive diver and swimmer. His best stroke, the butterfly, was nothing but pure gross motor movement, as he described it. It could withstand any amount of adrenaline that got pumped through the body's large muscles. He reveled in the feeling that adrenaline gave him in the water. That's where he could work with it. But all pleasure vanished as soon as he climbed the diving board. There, he turned erratic—sometimes dazzling, sometimes embarrassing, often hitting the hardest dives while missing the easiest ones.

"That's what I was like at the piano," I interrupted.

"Everyone tells you to just relax, but if that's all it took, it would be a piece of cake," he said. Kageyama had told me the same thing. Both taught that adrenaline is invaluable to performance. It just has to be channeled. "Because as soon as the adrenaline kicks in, you can't relax. You can try to relax before you perform, and sometimes it helps. But once you get into the music and the adrenaline spikes, you're blindsided."

As a young child, Greene had a speech impediment that prevented him from articulating his r's, making the pronunciation of his last name a fearsome challenge. The other kids laughed at him. He dreaded being called on in class and never raised his hand. One of his worst memories from his four years at the United States Military Academy at West Point was the five-minute presentation he was required to give for a revolutionary warfare seminar. The subject was Che Guevara, whose fearlessness fascinated Greene. His audience consisted of eight classmates, the same senior cadets he had "been through heaven and hell with. More heaven than hell." He prepared, overprepared, and lost three or four nights' sleep to worry. As soon as he stood up to speak, he stuttered, choked, and grew flushed in the face. "I guess I must have got to the end because I graduated," he said. The details have been pushed aside in memory, but a few weeks later he turned down an opportunity to attend law school because he couldn't imagine ever speaking in front of a jury. That's when he decided to become a psychologist. He wanted to understand what happened to him under pressure. Why had he been such an erratic springboard diver? Why did he still run for the hills whenever he had to speak before a small group of colleagues?

By the time I called him, he had been shuttling back and forth between music and sports for the past fifteen years. One of his sports success stories was Brigitte Foster-Hylton, the Jamaican track star who suffered a series of disappointing performances in the 100-meter hurdles. When Greene met her, she was already thirty-four, practically a senior citizen in a sport like the hurdles. She was training to compete in the 2009 World Championships in Berlin, and Greene's first impression of her was typically blunt: "In spite of her college degree and years competing at the highest levels in her event for many years, she didn't know how to use her mind to win." But he was impressed by her motivation and work ethic. He trained with her in New York and Kingston, Jamaica, where she ran on a track littered with weeds and trash. That was where he spotted a problematic behavior. Whenever she approached the hurdle, her eyes dropped and focused on the ground in front. Though she didn't realize it, it was throwing off her body position and stride. Under Greene's guidance, she changed her posture, learning to keep her head up and eyes focused on the space above the next hurdle. He gave her the handouts that by then he had developed for his Juilliard students, explaining how to focus, visualize, and move back and forth between left and right brain. They worked on breathing, centering, and prerace routines. A couple of months later in Berlin, she became the world champion and went on to win seven more major competitions at the unheard-of age of thirty-five.

But while Greene guided Foster-Hylton and others to victory, he berated himself for what he termed his "two big failures" of recent memory. The first happened when he was trying to sell his house in California. Thinking to save himself some money by selling it independently, he went to a meeting where he was invited to pitch potential home buyers about the sale. He choked. The second time happened at Juilliard, when he was asked to explain his coaching style in a two-minute presentation before faculty and students. He had been busy all week and didn't prepare. "It was terrible," he remembered. "I was very embarrassed, uncomfortable to the point where I have trouble talking about it even now."

"I can relate," I began to confide, but he was on a roll. Performance wasn't about being comfortable. If you want to be comfortable, stay home and play your piano in a sound-proofed room. But learn to channel your adrenaline flow and you'll give a high-energy performance. Dismissively, he said that all the young musicians he met were either meditating or medicating away their anxiety.

"That's what I've been doing," I blurted.

He didn't seem surprised. "I want my people to have high energy," he said flatly. "Everybody else is trying to relax and calm themselves with beta-blockers. Not my students."

"But how do you learn to get past that?" I asked.

"Do you really want to know how?" he asked. "I'll teach you."

Chapter 13

TEST DRIVE

I BEGAN WORKING WITH sport psychologist Don Greene in early May, ten days before my solo recital at the downtown library. I had committed to this recital months earlier, imagining it as a dress rehearsal for the real deal. Now, as it approached, I worried that I'd underestimated the event. It was part of a monthly series presenting local musicians, both professional and semiprofessional. Lots of people would show up. It was advertised on the radio and drew a devoted following of retirees, office workers, and fellow musicians. If anything, I was beginning to think that this recital was the litmus test. I had underplayed its import, in part because of its cheesy name, Munching with Mozart, but also because the library, any library, to me represented a safe haven. I'd spent so many hours inside this one that I knew most of the librarians and recognized quite a few of the homeless people who read and napped at its tables.

As I explained all this to Greene, he cut me off. "Let me prepare you for this fight," he said. "So you don't go into the ring and get beat up." Clearly, I was now under the tutelage of a sport psychologist and the metaphors had changed. I had found Greene in San Diego, where he'd recently moved to work with the USA Track & Field Team. Not all the athletes were buying what he had to teach, however, and it would be weeks before the International Olympic Committee decided whether it wanted what he was selling: the performance inventory he'd staked his life on. While he was waiting for the verdict (a resounding yes), he would amuse himself with me. But first I had to fill out his inventory, his Bible, the version he adapted for musicians. I had filled out something similar for Noa Kageyama nearly a year earlier, but Greene was insistent that he consider my profile through fresh eyes.

It took about an hour to complete, but I could tell at once that my responses had changed in the past year. I'd been toughened by all those trial runs: the evening soirees at my house, the master classes, the piano teacher recitals, piano camp recitals, and airport recitals. After months of demanding lessons and four- and five-hour daily practice sessions, my musical confidence was higher than it had ever been. Sometimes, as I heard myself at the piano, I felt pretty pleased with myself. So while I didn't anticipate it was going to be a slam dunk, I was taken aback when Greene called with the results.

"Your left brain is alive and well," he announced in his clipped Long Island accent. "Unfortunately, this performance is a right brain activity. You're setting yourself up for a left brain show." I'd been thinking so much about the details—articulation, dynamics, voicing, pedaling—that I was in overthink. Once, at my lesson, when I complained about lack of focus, my teacher had stared at me and told me my problem was hyperfocus. I knew, of course, that an active left brain meant tighter muscles and a louder internal critic, but Greene put it to me in stark terms. "It means that you can do quite well for some period of time. But with a feeling of danger, a slip in focus—you make a mistake and the committee's going to come in." My own panel of judges, he meant. "And you won't recover." The key to performance, he declared, was all in the right brain.

I wondered aloud if I even had a right brain, which he found funny. But in truth, my body was filled with clues of left brain dominance. At the piano, I was most definitely a righty player. After years of practicing yoga, my right leg was still a fraction longer than the left, and the right side of my back was significantly stronger. Such lopsidedness is far from uncommon. There is a whole science dedicated to the asymmetry of body and brain. According to one evolutionary theory, the predilection for right-handedness can be traced to ancient times, when women, the primary hunters, carried their babies in their left arms, where the sound of the heart soothed and quieted the infant. Ultrasound studies have found a strong preference for right-handedness (that is, left brain dominance) in the womb. From fifteen weeks of gestation, the typical fetus sucks on the right thumb; from thirty-eight weeks of gestation, it shows a preference for turning its head to the right. A whole body of research identifies "pathological left-handedness" as a consequence of prenatal stress. Studies, some discredited, have found that left-handed people were more likely to suffer from immune disorders, dyslexia, epilepsy, autism, and schizophrenia. More recent studies suggest that left-handedness may actually confer intellectual advantage. A sample of elementary school children found a correlation between left-handedness and high IQ scores. A 2013 review of research into handedness and cognition found that the main predictor of cognitive performance isn't whether an individual is left-handed or right-handed. It is determined by the strength of the preference. The more ambidextrous one is, the more communication there is between the brain's hemispheres, leading to better intellectual performance.

I was never going to be a lefty, but I realized that Greene was correct: I needed to find a way to switch to the right brain—and stay there—throughout the performance. He was telling me exactly what Kageyama had told me. It was all about centering. "Never again—not in your sleep, not in your thoughts—are you to sit down at the piano without first forming an intent and centering. Center before your lesson. Center before you begin to practice. Center before the library recital."

In construction, centering refers to the temporary wooden framework used to build an arch or dome; it's responsible for the integrity of the structure. At the potter's wheel, centering is that process from which all growth and potential arise in the clay. Psychologists use the word *centering* to describe the act of coming into a state where the mind is focused yet relaxed. Yoga teachers talk about a centered state of balance between body and mind, while folklorists talk about the navel of the world. In a 1985 interview, Joseph Campbell, de facto expert on the world's mythology, put it this way: "The function of mythological symbols is to give you a sense of 'Aha! Yes. I know what it is, it's myself.' This is what it's all about, and then you feel a kind of centering, centering, centering all the time."

Greene cited research that found an increase of alpha waves almost always precedes a fully centered peak performance. It was all rather confusing. The biofeedback program I played with months before had measured beta waves, which are associated with active thinking and concentration. Richard Davidson, the neuroscientist, extolled the benefit of gamma waves for changing brain function and improving attentiveness. Now here was Greene talking about alpha waves, which he called "the gateway to the subconscious." According to one study he quoted, elite golfers produce a burst of alpha waves before hitting their best shots. The left brain goes into hibernation; verbal thought comes to a grinding halt; the right brain takes over.

As we began to work—one hour every morning by phone—it would take me thirty or forty seconds to locate my center, and even then I wouldn't be sure I'd really found it. Standing up, I would imagine a Hula-Hoop rotating around my hips. I would try to sense where it lay, two inches below the navel and two inches deep inside me, according to Greene. "But pinpointing its precise location is not as important as getting out of your head and focusing your energy down." After a few days, I could find it in five or ten seconds—sitting at the piano, gaze focused just below eye level. If your eyes move upward, it usually means you're engaging in left brain thinking.

I centered at the kitchen table while looking over the piano score and playing the music in my head. ("If you make a mistake, stop the 'tape,' rewind, and do it again," Greene advised.) I centered while playing my scales. ("Slowly, like a new student. Imagine a concert stage, a huge Steinway, and this elephant comes walking out in a purple polka-dot bathing suit, sits down at the piano, adjusts the pedal, and starts playing Rachmaninoff flawlessly. If you can imagine that, you're in right brain.") I centered before my lesson. ("There's no reason for you to play until you're ready to play. And that means centering. Switch to right brain, hear the first few bars, and play. Feel it. See it. Hear it.")

Don Greene (Courtesy of Larny Mack)

All those years of military training, at West Point, in the U.S. Army, as a Green Beret, had given Greene a commanding manner, and he gave instructions like orders. I welcomed the imperative. His style grounded the trendy spirituality that lay at the heart of his teachings. Though his advice wasn't new, I sometimes felt as if I were hearing it for the first time. Centering would give me the ability to play freely, not perfectly. Perfection was an illusion, I reminded myself. Besides, in and of itself, it was boring. I'd attended so many boring concerts over the years, concerts that were exercises in perfection. As a listener, I craved excitement and discovery. It's our faults and mistakes that provide guideposts to our higher capabilities. "People want to hear excitement," Greene agreed. "They want to hear energy. When you play it safe, when every detail is perfect, chances are it isn't exciting. It's like a tennis player who makes every serve. They're not playing at the edge of their capabilities. Until they start faulting, they don't know how much range they have for faster serves."

Take risks. Push the edge. Wondering what it would take to jar me out of my comfort zone, I thought of what had happened to my friend Mary, who in her twenties was dining at a fancy restaurant when she choked on a piece of meat. Her face swelled and turned beet red as she gagged for breath. Her date stared at her, frozen. She gestured down at her rib cage: Didn't he know the Heimlich maneuver? He reached across, as if waking from a dream, and grabbed her by the breasts. Mary gasped in shock, and the chunk of meat flew out of her mouth and across the table. Somehow I, too, needed to be saved.

"No more negative self-talk," Greene ordered. "What you think is what you get. What you fear is what you attract." Nobody needed to convince me about the power of the mind, but when Greene warned me that my fear could manifest its very object, something in me fought back. "Banish all doubt!" he advised, to which I mutely answered, "Ye who enter here."

"You've been watching the same negative horror films for too long," he insisted. "Burn them. Let them go."

Day after day we talked, and as the library recital got closer, the conversations got longer. The process was repetitive and exhausting, and I sometimes wondered whether my time would be better spent at the piano. Greene sensed my doubts. "I'm used to resistance," he said. "There are two things holding you back, and that's fear and negative thinking."

That was hard to argue. All I had learned and practiced over the past year—the psychological insights, the meditation, not to mention the Brahms, the Bach, and the Debussy— hardly mattered if I couldn't break through my wall of fear. I had to believe in myself enough to stand before an assembly and demand its attention. To say, *Listen to me as I speak through this music.* To assert, *I have something to say.*

I had, for the first time in my life, begun reading self-help books. *The Magic of Thinking Big. The Tools. Live Your Truth. The Power of Intention.* I began each one thinking it might have something unique to tell me, some nugget I was missing and hadn't understood: a secret truth that would be as eye-opening and revelatory as a grab for the breasts.

None of them helped me as much as one of my last conversations with Greene. "How many years have you been playing?" he asked as we approached the ten-day mark. "How many lessons have you had? You're well trained. You're a good student. With my help, with Noa's help, it's going to go well. You can do anything you set your mind to. If you took up rock climbing, I'm sure you'd figure that out. But my money's on you with the piano. Say it with conviction: It's going to go well."

That was what he said to me the day before my recital, but the words that stuck were: "You can do anything you set your mind to." I recognized those words. They were the very words my mother said to me throughout my childhood, into my adulthood, and well into her senility. They were the words that brought me full circle.

The night before the library recital, I scribbled a detailed description of how I wanted it to go. No, not "wanted." Intended. Want, as Greene informed me, was a dysfunctional word. "Wanting creates more wanting. Life is not a discovery. It's a creation." There was a time I would have dismissed this as just another platitude, but now I embraced it as a motto, another good-luck charm for my growing stockpile. My most important charm was the blurry black-and-white photograph of my late aunty Maddy—my quintessential audience—that I kept on the piano rack. Now a little wooden totem sat next to it. I placed it there after attending a workshop by Margret Elson, a pianist and psychotherapist in Oakland, California, who specialized in the problems of artists and performers. I liked her integrative approach and the way she used both physical prompts and meditation to help overcome stage fright. When she suggested that we use a cue or physical prompt to enter into a state of relaxation—hers was a polished green stone—I immediately recalled the totem that my best friend, Kathie, gave me in high school. For years, I wore it around my neck like an amulet. As soon as the workshop was done, I went home, found it in an old shoebox, and added it to my stockpile of talismans.

The morning of the library recital, my hands were cold and unresponsive as I warmed up at home. As I played slowly through my pieces, the errors mounted, and I was grateful that Greene had insisted on scheduling a final phone session. "It's going to go well," he assured me. "And no matter what happens, keep playing. If the legs of the piano fall off, keep playing. Never stop playing." I thought of Vladimir Horowitz's injunction as he accompanied the young Gitta Gradova to

Picture of Aunty Maddy that Sara kept on her piano
(Author's family photo)

a solo performance with the New York Philharmonic. "No matter what happens, *don't stop playing*!" the famously jittery Horowitz told her on the cab ride to Carnegie Hall. "Remember, no matter what happens, keep on going! Don't stop! *It's provincial to stop!*"[1] The last thing I wanted was to be provincial.

"I can do anything I set my mind to," I muttered as I climbed the stairs to the library's recital room, my husband, Rich, and son Max in tow. They'd been hearing a lot of these affirmations over the past few days and offered some of their own. "I love to play with you, Mom," Max said. He was joining me for a Haydn violin sonata, the first piece on the program. "It's going to go well," I said to myself, sounding a little grim. The recital room was adjacent to the children's room, where I'd spent so many contented hours, searching (unobserved, I now remembered wistfully) for books, with Max, then a toddler, curling up in my lap at story time. I stared at the piano, a decent upright that I had tried out a couple of days earlier to get a feel for the keys and the acoustics of the room. Now as I sat down to warm up, half a dozen mothers and children wandered in to listen. It made a nice first audience. Rich set up his iPad to record the recital, and when I looked up a moment later, there was Lynn Kidder, my erstwhile coach. She wore a huge smile. She had heard me play through my pieces a few days before and, if anything, was more positive than Don Greene. I was a different pianist from the one she had met a year ago, she said. Rich, of course, had told me the same, but he was my husband and I wasn't sure I could believe him.

Kidder led me to a backroom corridor, where she had posi-
tioned a couple of chairs. She wanted to share a preperform-
ance ritual with me. I had accumulated so many performance
rituals by this point: the photograph, the totem, the belly
breathing, the beta-blocker. Oh wait! I forgot to take my
beta-blocker. I should have taken it at least an hour ago; now,
it was only twenty minutes to showtime, not nearly enough
time for it to kick in. What if my hands turned wet and
clammy? What if my foot shook so badly that I couldn't
control the pedals? What if I was poisoned by adrenaline? I
ran back to the recital room, where I'd left my handbag with
Rich, rooted around, found the prescription bottle, and
gulped down one of the little pills. Just another ritual, I told
myself, returning to the corridor where Kidder was waiting.
Following her lead, I crossed my left ankle over my right
knee, placed my right hand on my ankle and my left hand
under the ball of my left foot. Five long breaths, in through
the nose and out through the mouth. Then I did the same on
the opposite side. I made a tent with my fingertips and
smoothed my forehead, like wiping away the wrinkles. Max
leaned against the wall and watched. Now twenty-seven, he
had wrestled with his own bouts of stage fright. In his first
year of conservatory in Toronto, he was so undone by anxiety
that even his violin lessons became exercises in fear. He took
solace in knowing that several of his teachers and coaches over
the years had their own problems with stage fright. One was
so cocky about his abilities that he hardly read over his solo
before a rehearsal with a major orchestra. When on one occasion he flubbed his part, he felt so mortified that he was never

again able to play in public without a beta-blocker. What was the harm in a beta-blocker?

I breathed deep belly breaths, and now, with the door to the recital room open just a crack, I heard the announcement of my name and the applause of the audience. It was time. "People don't enjoy watching someone playing like they're being led to the gallows," Greene had admonished. I walked through the door, Max behind me, Kidder, my page-turner, behind him. And there was my teacher, Ellen Chen, in the second row, next to my friend Mary. They were both beaming. I bowed and smiled at the audience. Maybe I should have taken a longer bow? Would I never stop second-guessing myself? Yes, but wasn't it Michael Tilson Thomas, conductor of the San Francisco Symphony, who said that coming out onstage and bowing was the hardest part of his job? Stop! I commanded myself. Shut up.

I sat at the piano and looked at Max, whose violin was raised and ready. I stared down at the lettering on the fall board of the piano—a Knabe. Just below eye level. I waited. I centered. There was no hurry. It was like that long, sustained moment when you're at the top of the roller coaster after the slow climb up the tracks, and you wait for the gravitational pull that sweeps you down with all that energy and danger. I can do anything I set my mind to, I told myself one last time. I took a deep breath. *Fasten your seat belts*, I wanted to shout.

I gave a sharp nod at Max and we launched into the Haydn. It was at once fluid and easy. Halfway through, I skipped a bar. Max understood instantly and jumped ahead to meet me. Such a maestro, I thought, and felt an outpouring of love and gratitude for my middle son. It was so comforting to accompany him, to play in the background and let him sing. The second movement was a soft adagio. I felt myself relaxing into the music, which was so plaintive, so clear, so goddamn lovely. Was that a little mistake I'd made? I wasn't sure and I didn't care. I sang the notes in my head as I played, and when, too soon, it was over, all I wanted was to hear the music again. I think I yearned to hear it more than I yearned to play it. When the applause began, I felt stunned, the way you feel after awakening from an unexpected nap. Max and I hadn't planned how we would take our bows, but we naturally linked arms and bowed clumsily.

Now it was just me and the piano. I had intended to start with the Bach Prelude and Fugue in C Minor, but there was something about Bach that made me feel exposed. I changed the order of the music and began with Debussy's *Reflets dans l'eau*. I took another deep breath, let it out slowly, and reached for my center. Was that it? I waited and searched for that evanescent sense of core. Yes, there it was. I breathed into it and began—a music of dreams, a feeling of fluidity beneath my fingers, of reflections rippling in the water and moving within the keys. I thought, perhaps, there was a glitch in a crescendo of arpeggios, but it was soon far behind me, like a branch in white-water rapids. Deep in the rhythm of it, I told myself to just sing. The runs were softer, faster, more liquid, than any I could remember having played before. A thought broke through the ripples: I'm doing very well, I wonder what people think of me? I swatted it away like a gnat. And then, almost as soon as it had begun, it, too, was over. Between pieces, I could hear the hum of a happy audience, which sounded to my ears like the hum of diners at a restaurant. I was having fun. Starting the Brahms rhapsody, I felt under a spell, watching my fingers moving over the keys. I seemed to drift like a balloonist above the room until there were no more notes to play and I came down for a landing, wishing I could keep going. As the applause began, I had an urge to raise a hand and tell my audience, *Wait, I can play more.* I looked over at my husband and realized that he was tearing up. I smiled at my teacher, who was grinning. A five-year-old girl laid her head on her grandmother's shoulder and said loudly, "This is just like *Young Einstein.*" I was elated. I had never played so well.

Chapter 14

FINALE

IT WAS JUNE 30, 2013, and I was lying on the only available floor space in the green room, a Sunday school office in the basement of Christ Lutheran Church, just a few miles from my house. I stared up at the shelves crammed with Bibles, children's activity books, and boxes of colored pencils, reminding myself to breathe and center. Directly overhead, a growing hum of voices filled my ears like the slow roar of the earthquake that ran through my house in 1989, announcing itself like the New York subway. There had even been a long suspended moment during which I wondered stupidly what the subway was doing under my house on the California coast. It was a flimsy house back then; we called it the Jolly Roger because of the shredded canvas awnings that flapped around on the decks. By the time I realized what was happening—not just an earthquake, but the promised Big One—the ground was shaking and I was screaming for my children, running down the hall, flung bodily from wall to wall. The exhilaration of survival stayed with me for days afterward. Now I anticipated that my performance, for which I'd been preparing the past year, would also exhilarate. I was pretty confident that I would survive.

A week after the library recital in May, my teacher had flown to Shanghai to see her husband. During her absence, she arranged for me to perform for two of her colleagues. One was a retired Argentinian pianist in long floral robes named Celia Mendez; the other was Ellen's own duet partner, Tom Burns. I played through my entire repertoire for each of them, and they gave me hours of undivided attention. I left their studios, my head spinning with suggestions, criticisms, and interpretations regarding tempo, articulation, pedaling, and the length of my fermatas, or pauses. I drove two hours to Berkeley for yet another lesson with Gwendolyn Mok, the concert pianist who had urged me to go for excellence instead of perfection. A demanding pedagogue, Mok was known for her wit and her insights, which could be acerbic. A friend of mine, knowing how thin-skinned I could be about the piano, questioned whether I really needed to subject myself to Mok's scrutiny.

The answer was yes. I was feeling a lot more assured about my playing, and I wanted to know what she thought. She had recently recorded a collection of Brahms's piano music and had strong ideas about how he should be approached. After I played through the Romanze in F Major, she pointed to the inner voicings—not the soprano line I'd been drawing out, but the alto and tenor lines, which, she believed, symbolized the secret love of Brahms and Clara Schumann. "And don't brace your shoulders," she cautioned as I furiously took notes. "When you play an octave, you stick your boobs out. That's not going to help." I had to find the hydraulics in my hands, flatten them like pancakes, and then raise them, elevator style, like an old Citroën automobile.

I was still making sense of everything she and the others had told me when Ellen returned to California. She had cut short her stay in China to fly back and hear me one last time before my concert. She never got jet lag, she said, dismissing my hesitation about scheduling a lesson a few hours after her touchdown in San Jose. She would be ready to go after a brief nap. All she asked for was a wake-up call on my way over "the hill." I remembered to call her at the summit. The phone rang and rang until finally she picked up, her voice cracked with sleep and not all that pleased to hear me. "Is there any way we can reschedule?" she asked. I had just passed the last turnoff on Highway 17, and there wouldn't be another one until I reached the base of the mountain, not far from her house. My concert was four days away. "Oh, just come over," she capitulated. "Drive slow. I'll make some strong coffee."

She hadn't heard me play for nearly a month, and I began with the rhapsody. I knew I had had a breakthrough these last few weeks, but I wasn't prepared for Ellen's response. She set down her coffee, stared at me, and passed her hands across her heart. "You are at a whole other level," she declared. I played *Reflets dans l'eau*, and when I finished, she shook her head. "You have had a transformation." It happened with each piece I played, and when I was done she stood up and seemed to search for what she wanted to say. "You are a different pianist from the last time I heard you."

Now, lying on the floor of the Sunday School office, my chartreuse dress smoothed beneath me, I told myself I had every reason for confidence. I had chosen each piece on my program because I loved it. The program was ambitious, an hour's worth of music, nearly twice what I played at the library, and I intended to communicate my love for this music, perhaps to make converts of people who wouldn't otherwise hear it, like my friends who listened mostly to Bob Marley and Jimmy Buffett. I wanted to keep Bach and Brahms alive. In the late 1960s, in the heat of my infatuation with Glenn Gould, I'd worn out the grooves listening to his recording of Bach's *Well-Tempered Clavier*, studying the cover, gazing into those brooding, leonine eyes—never guessing that the reason behind his repudiation of live performance was most likely stage fright. Now here I was, about to perform the Prelude and Fugue in C Minor, one of my favorites from the *Well-Tempered Clavier*.

"Are you ready, Mom?" Max asked. I raised myself up off the floor. I was as ready as I would ever be. He led the way up a flight of stairs into the octagonal sanctuary. It wasn't far from a noisy interchange on Highway 1, but the sanctuary was an oasis of quiet and the bank of stained-glass windows cast the soft light of a forest canopy. I'd spent a couple of hours in the room over the previous week, familiarizing myself with the Yamaha grand piano, moseying around the pews, getting comfortable in the space. Entering it now, I moved past a crowd of faces that appeared to me as unfocused as a drive-by blur. These were my children, my family, and my friends, some of whom had come from the East Coast, the Rocky Mountains, Hawaii, and Canada. I picked out my sister, Syma, who more than almost anyone understood what this occasion meant to me. I tried to make out my friend Amy, who had flown in from Montana, but my eyes clouded over. It was time to take a bow, and I made it quick. I sat down at the piano, made eye contact with Max, and jumped into the Haydn. I forgot to center. I forgot to let in—what had Landis Gwynn called it?—the sacredness. I just played. And for a while it was okay. Then I lost it. My breath hung in the air. My fingers screeched to a halt. My heart was in my mouth. What a cliché. But it wasn't just my heart. All my vital organs had moved up and lay at the base of my throat. *Remember, no matter what happens, keep on going! Don't stop!* Lynn Kidder, my page-turner, my Virgil, laid her fingers on the page and I was back.

With Haydn over, Max walked off and I heard Don Greene's command. *Never again—not in your sleep, not in your thoughts—are you to sit down at the piano without centering.* Alone, I centered. *Feel it. See it. Hear it.* I heard the first few bars of the Bach prelude and knew how I would play them. Landis, my former teacher, had cautioned me to take it slower than I was accustomed, but as I began the prelude I paid no mind to prudence. I had a passion for this piece, which struck me as simultaneously rational and emotional, Apollonian and Dionysian. It demanded utter control, yet it was a wild piece with a tension that advanced and uncoiled until it reached the point where all hell broke loose. After so many months of practicing and deconstructing its mysteries, I had the tech-nique to play it as I heard it, and my intent was to turn loose its ferocity. Now I felt my fingers run through the familiar patterns and had the image of a tightrope. But I wasn't walking a tightrope; I was running it. I came to the pause, the silence before the fast and furious presto. My eyes flickered across the page, which looked more like a swarm of ants than the music I so thoroughly knew. It was a Hansel and Gretel moment—I was lost—but then, yes, I spotted the crumbs leading back to the path. I finished with a false sense of gusto and continued on to the fugue. A feeling of dispiritedness moved through me: disappointment; a taste of bile. I paused for a long moment before starting the rhapsody, then exhaled so loudly that I thought I heard an echo. The acoustics of the room were excellent.

Months before, Ellen had assured me that one day this would be my signature piece. I loved it for its sheer physical-ity: its two-octave leaps, the repeated crossings of the left hand over the right, and the sonorous heavy chords. It was like wrestling a grizzly bear. It was the most majestic piece I had ever played. The emotion it unleashed was practically excruciating; Brahms's yearning and perseverance seemed to cry out from every note. I forgot the audience and aligned myself with its fierceness and introspection. By the time I moved on to Debussy's *Suite Bergamasque*, the music took over. *Feel it. See it. Hear it.* The prelude was otherworldly, a reprieve from the intensity of Brahms. The music was falling into place, and I hardly had to do anything except follow it.

It was only after my encore—a tango by the Argentinian Astor Piazzolla—that I allowed myself to look around the room, settling on faces, including that of my oldest son, Ben, seated in the front row with his partner, Amanda. They had flown in from Maui for my big day, but—befogged by Brahms—I hadn't noticed them until that moment. Handing me a bouquet of

Ellen and Sara after the recital (Ted Lorraine)

white roses, Ben gave me a hug, and I can vaguely remember the roomful of people on their feet. My eyes combed the room, as if maybe, in my heart of hearts, I expected to spot my mother, a younger version of the one I'd last known, sitting tall and erect, chin jutted, clearly proud of me, forgiving of my mistakes—while also fully cognizant of how many I had made.

Back at the house, I celebrated my sixtieth birthday with a party, but I felt bereft. Now what? For days, I brooded about whether I had fallen short of my goal. I was reluctant to listen to the recording of the concert, afraid of what I would hear. I remembered how I once used to avoid checking my bank balance, certain I would find it in the red. But when I finally broke down and listened to my concert, I was surprised. I heard some lapses, yes. But I also heard expressiveness. I heard assertiveness. I heard a voice. What I heard was me, Sara: I was not a professional, and I was hardly perfect. But I was striving for excellence, and sometimes I attained it.

My father had once told me that the best way to understand something about myself was to try to change it. (In my memory, he was alluding to my bad habit of biting my nails. It drove him crazy.) He was obsessed with the idea of change, probably because he was so resistant to change himself. He lectured us kids about it constantly—usually to impress upon us the intractability of personality. He relished the Jesuit maxim "Give me the boy until he is seven and I will show you the man"—though in my father's opinion, the magic age was more like two. But he was an inconsistent man, so he also told us that the best way to try to understand something is to try to change it. I would take those words to heart, though it was years before I discovered that my stubborn dad was quoting Kurt Lewin, the social psychologist famous for his theories on the human potential for change.

Lewin's model was based on three stages: "unfreezing, changing, and freezing." The first stage, "unfreezing," begins with the recognition that a change is required. (In my case, it was time for me to face my demons.) Once a person accepts that imperative, she has to overcome her inertia (I had to declare my intent, find the right teacher, ratchet up my practicing) and dismantle her previous "mind-set" (my conviction that I was not a performer, that maybe I wasn't even a real pianist). The second stage is where "change" actually occurs. It's not a single event; it's a period of transition, a process that generates confusion and even chaos. (I perform, make mistakes, feel chagrined, but learn to survive and accept imperfection.) In the third stage, known as "freezing" or "refreezing," the change is crystallized and becomes the new norm. The journey has come to an end. (I can settle in and congratulate myself on a job well done. I'm a performer now.)

Which is where I part ways with Lewin. Conquering stage fright isn't like planting a flag on the moon. The journey doesn't end so definitively. In important ways, it doesn't end at all. For me, the act of getting up and playing before an audience is something I'll wrestle with for as long as I play the piano.

Looking back, I see the gap that's always existed between who I think I am and the reality of what I am. Forty years ago, as an au pair in Italy, I happened to find a letter written by the signora, describing me as *"gentile, pero poco timida"*—nice, but a little shy. Her opinion shocked me. I—the loudmouth of my family, the one who fought and won most dinnertime debates, if only through the force of my voice—*timida?* My private and public personae were more different than I wished to admit.

We all dance so freely when alone in our bedrooms. The danger lies in stepping out from behind the closed door. Early in my year's journey, I heard of a man who hoarded five pianos, two of them grands, in a double-wide trailer. He refused to play for anybody but himself; he collected pianos the way some people collect figurines. The image of those imprisoned pianos haunted me. It seemed pathetic, his music making like the proverbial tree falling in the forest. What was the good of all that music if there was no one to hear it? The image spurred me on to break out of my own double-wide trailer.

I'm out.

ACKNOWLEDGMENTS

A few years ago I was visiting my friend Amy Linn in Missoula when, deep into a bottle of wine, we began swapping stories about stage fright. I described my piano disasters, she told me about her equestrian ones. That conversation set in motion a project that would consume me for the next three years. Amy's smarts and creative vision have inspired me from the beginning. Her early readings were invaluable, and when I got lost in a thicket of words, she helped me find my way out.

This project leaned on the expertise of many different people, beginning with my piano teachers: Landis Gwynn, whose uncontained passion for Bach and Beethoven first brought me back to classical music; Lynn Kidder, my ballast whenever I feared I was reaching too high; and especially Ellen Tryba Chen, who pushed, prodded, and refused to accept anything less than excellence. Or at least my version of it.

Sport psychologist Noa Kageyama was incredibly generous, coaching me in weekly sessions that went on for months. Don Greene emerged in the final stages of my journey and gave me a mysterious boost that I still wonder at. Other psychologists, notably John Beebe, Susan Raeburn, and Ron Thompson, gave freely of their time and insights. And I benefited from the wisdom of several concert pianists: Frederic Chiu, Gwendolyn Mok, and Ruth Slenczynska, who shared their thoughts and stories about the act of performing. I'm also grateful to John Orlando, whose fearless reflections on a lifetime of performance anxiety touched me deeply.

Many friends and family read the manuscript in its various permutations. My gratitude goes to Amy Beddoe, Irene Borger, Jennifer Eberhardt, Donka Farkas, and Jill Wolfson. A big thank-you to Mary Offermann, who not only read every word and questioned every comma, but also listened to me expound on my latest piano discovery on our weekly rain-or-shine trip to the Santa Cruz farmers' market. Thanks also to Jim LaMarche and Christine Z. Mason for being willing to step in and help at a minute's notice. Debbie Katz appeared at a critical juncture and gave enormous support and encouragement. And a special thank-you to Kit Seelye, whose critical eye and sound judgment have kept me honest for the past thirty years.

Thanks to my agent, Michael Bourrett, who shepherded this book from the initial query, and my editor, Jacqueline Johnson, whose judgments about style and organization have proven correct time and again. Every author should have an editor like her.

Thank you to my sister, Syma Solovitch, who read, laughed, and assured me that "Mummy would have loved it." Her caring, intelligence, and rapier wit nurtured me throughout the final stages. My brother, Joseph—always an anchor—helped me recall details of childhood. A big thank-you to my sons, Ben, Max, and Jesse, whose self-aplomb onstage set a high standard. My favorite music making has always been with them. As an editor, Max has an eye for detail that is as sharp and nuanced as his aptitude for memorizing a Bach partita.

And last, but most of all, to Rich, for whom there are no words. He knows.

NOTES

Introduction

1 Hugh Grant interview, *Entertainment Weekly*, August 14, 2009; Paul McCartney interview, *NME*, November 25, 2009; Adele interview, *Rolling Stone*, April 28, 2011; Christopher Nupen, *Andrés Segovia: In Portrait* (Guildford, UK: Allegro Films, 2012); Elizabeth Silverthorne, *Sarah Bernhardt* (Philadelphia: Chelsea House Publishing, 2003), 47; David Amos, "Horowitz, Other Greats, Suffered from Stage Fright," *San Diego Jewish World*, May 23, 2014.

2 Anne Edwards, *Streisand: A Biography* (Boston: Little, Brown, 1997); Laurence Olivier, *Confessions of an Actor: An Autobiography* (New York: Simon & Schuster, 1985); Richard David Story, Nightlife, *New York Magazine*, September 13, 1993; Marianne Bahmann, *Coping with the Limelight: A Manual on Stage Fright* (n.p.: BookSurge, 2009); John Lahr, "Petrified," *New Yorker*, August 28, 2006, 38–42; Phillip D. Atteberry, "Remembering Ella,"

Mississippi Rag, April 1996; Alan Zilberman, "Interview: Jesse Eisenberg Talks About 'Now You See Me' and Never Watching Movies," *Washington City Paper*, May 23, 2013; Joseph Murphy, *The Power of Your Subconscious Mind* (Radford, Va.: Wilder Publications, 2008); NBC News, September 12, 2007, http://www.nbcnews.com/id/20727420/ns/health-mental_health/t/even-stars-get-stage-fright/; "About This Person: Movies & TV," http://www.nytimes.com/movies/person/91479/Mel-Gibson/biography; Ronald Blum, "Luciano Pavarotti: A Tenor Like No Other," *USA Today*, September 6, 2007; Alexis Petridis, "The Astonishing Genius of Brian Wilson," *Guardian*, June 24, 2011 http://www.theguardian.com/music/2011/jun/24/brian-wilson-interview; Carol Burnett, *This Time Together: Laughter and Reflection* (New York: Crown Publishing Group, 2010).

3　　"What Are Americans Afraid Of?," *Bruskin Report* 53 (July 1973).

Chapter 2: BLINDED BY THE LIGHT: A SHORT HISTORY

1　　Exodus 4:10–16.

2　　Carl Gustav Jung, *Visions: Notes of the Seminar Given in 1930–1934*, vol. 1, ed. Claire Douglas (Princeton, N.J.: Princeton University Press, 1997).

3　　Mark Twain, *The Adventures of Tom Sawyer* (New York: Scholastic Paperbacks, 1999), 196.

4 Jay-Z, *Fresh Air*, NPR, November 16, 2010, http://www
   .npr.org/2010/11/16/131334322/the-fresh-air-interview-
   jay-z-decoded.

5 Jon McKenzie, *Perform or Else: From Discipline to
   Performance* (New York: Routledge, 2001), 3.

6 Glen O. Gabbard, "Stage Fright," *International Journal of
   Psychoanalysis* 60 (1979): 383.

7 Susan Dominus, "What Happened to the Girls in Le
   Roy," *New York Times Magazine*, March 7, 2012.

8 Quentin Letts, "The Terror That Turns Our Acting
   Giants to Jelly," *Daily Mail*, August 27, 2013.

9 Harry Lee Poe and Rebecca Whitten Poe, eds., *The
   Good, the True, and the Beautiful: Meditations* (St. Louis,
   Mo.: Chalice Press, 2008).

10 Nicholas Ridout, *Stage Fright, Animals, and Other
   Theatrical Problems* (New York: Cambridge University
   Press, 2006), 52.

11 Constantin Stanislavski, *An Actor Prepares*, trans.
   Elizabeth Reynolds Hapgood (New York: Theatre Arts
   Books, 1973).

12 Stephen Aaron, *Stage Fright: Its Role in Acting* (Chicago:
   University of Chicago Press, 1986), 122–23.

Chapter 3: TOUCHING A TARANTULA

1 Lahr, "Petrified," 36–42.

2 Arthur Golden, *Memoirs of a Geisha: A Novel* (New
   York: Vintage Books, 1999), 144.

3   Charles Rosen, *Critical Entertainments: Music Old and New* (Cambridge, Mass.: Harvard University Press, 2000), 9–10.

Chapter 6: REVENGE OF THE AMYGDALA

1   Robert D. Richardson, *William James: In the Maelstrom of American Modernism* (Boston: Houghton Mifflin, 2006), 237.

2   William James, "What Is an Emotion?," *Mind*, vol. 9, (1884): 188–205.

3   Joseph LeDoux, *The Emotional Brain: The Mysterious Underpinnings of Emotional Life* (New York: Simon & Schuster, 1996), 154.

4   James McGaugh, *Memory and Emotion: The Making of Lasting Memories* (New York: Columbia University Press, 2003).

5   LeDoux, *Emotional Brain*, 180–81.

6   Richard A. Gabriel, *No More Heroes: Madness and Psychiatry in War* (New York: Hill and Wang, 1987), 137.

7   Ibid., 139.

8   Nicolas Rasmussen, "Medical Science and the Military: The Allies' Use of Amphetamine During World War II," *Journal of Interdisciplinary History* 42, no. 2 (Autumn 2011): 205–33.

9   C. O. Brantigan, T. A. Brantigan, and N. Joseph, "Beta-Blockade and Musical Performance," *Lancet* 2 (October 21, 1978): 896.

10 C. O. Brantigan, T. A. Brantigan, and N. Joseph, "Effect of Beta Blockade and Beta Stimulation on Stage Fright," *American Journal of Medicine* 72 (January 1982).

Chapter 7: MIND GAMES

1 Bruno Monsaingeon, *Mademoiselle: Conversations with Nadia Boulanger* (Manchester, UK: Carcanet Press, 1985), 35.

2 Richard J. Davidson and Sharon Begley, *The Emotional Life of Your Brain* (New York: Hudson Street Press, 2012), 11.

3 Dianna T. Kenny, *The Psychology of Music Performance Anxiety* (Oxford: Oxford University Press, 2011), 268.

4 Davidson and Begley, *Emotional Life of Your Brain*, 167.

5 Ibid., 162.

Chapter 8: ME AND MY SHADOW

1 Jung, *Visions*, 1306.

2 Dorsha Hayes, "The Archetypal Nature of Stage Fright," *Art Psychotherapy* 2, nos. 3–4 (1975): 279–81.

3 Ruth Slenczynska and Louis Biancolli, *Forbidden Childhood* (Garden City, N.Y.: Doubleday & Co., 1957), 11.

4 Ibid., 48–49.

5 Ibid., 43.

6 Ibid., 58.

7   Ibid., 148.

8   Ibid., 202.

Chapter 9: SO MUCH FOR PERFECTION

1   Charles Nordhoff, *The Communistic Societies of the United States from Personal Visit and Observation* (New York: Harper & Brothers, 1875), 259–301.

2   Pierrepont Noyes, *My Father's House: An Oneida Boyhood* (New York: Farrar & Rinehart, 1937), 136.

3   Paul L. Hewitt and Gordon L. Flett, "When Does Conscientiousness Become Perfectionism?," *Current Psychiatry* 6, no. 7 (July 2007).

4   Jennifer Sey, *Chalked Up: My Life in Elite Gymnastics* (New York: HarperCollins, 2009).

5   Bonnie E. Robson, "Competition in Sport, Music and Dance," *Medical Problems of Performing Artists* 19, no. 4 (December 2004).

6   Donna Krasnow, Lynda Mainwaring, and Gretchen Kerr, "Injury, Stress, and Perfectionism in Young Dancers and Gymnasts," *Journal of Dance Medicine & Science* 3, no. 2 (1999): 51–58.

Chapter 10: UM . . . UM . . .

1   Karen Kangas Dwyer and Marlina M. Davidson, "Is Public Speaking Really More Feared Than Death?," *Communication Research Reports* 29, no. 2 (April–June 2012): 99–107.

2   James C. McCroskey, "Communication Apprehension: What Have We Learned in the Last Four Decades," *Human Communication* 12, no. 2 (n.d.): 157–71.

3   Henry Shukman, "The Art of Being Wrong," *Tricycle*, Spring 2013.

Chapter 11: CULTURAL ARTIFACTS OF FEAR

1   David Greenberg, Ariel Stravynski, and Yoram Bilu, "Social Phobia in Ultra-Orthodox Jewish Males; Culture-Bound Syndrome or Virtue?," *Mental Health, Religion & Culture* 7, no. 4 (2004): 289–305.

2   Stefan G. Hofmann, Anu Asnaani, and Devon E. Hinton, "Cultural Aspects in Social Anxiety and Social Anxiety Disorder," *Depression and Anxiety* 27, no. 12 (December 2010): 1117–27.

Chapter 12: GAME PLANS

1   Sian Beilock, *Choke: What the Secrets of the Brain Reveal About Getting It Right When You Have To* (New York: Free Press, 2010), 185.

Chapter 13: TEST DRIVE

1   Gary Graffman, *I Really Should Be Practicing* (New York: Doubleday & Co., 1981), 145.

INDEX

A NOTE ON THE AUTHOR

Sara Solovitch is a journalist who has been a medical writer at Stanford University and a reporter at the *Philadelphia Inquirer*. Her articles have appeared in the *Washington Post, Los Angeles Times, Esquire, Wired* and elsewhere. She lives in Santa Cruz, California. This is her first book.

www.sarasolo.com